THE CULTURAL HERITAGE OF JASNA GÓRA

THE CULTURAL HERITAGE

OF JASNA GÓRA

by Zofia Rozanow and Ewa Smulikowska
Photographs by Jan Michlewski
and Janusz Rosikoń
With an Introduction by Władysław Tomkiewicz

Interpress Publishers
Warsaw 1974

Translated by Stanisław Tarnowski
Designed by Stefan Bernaciński
Plan of Jasna Góra by Włodzimierz Galicki
Photographs by PA Interpress
Technical editor: Edward Kubiak
This is the one thousand three hundred and thirty-ninth publication of
Interpress Publishers
This book appears also in Polish
Printed in Poland
Illustrations printed by
Zakłady Wklęsłodrukowe — Warszawa
Set, printed and bound at
Prasowe Zakłady Graficzne — Wrocław

HE name of Jasna Góra is so well known that it surely requires no further explanation. I have no doubt that even Poles who left the country in their early youth, and those born abroad who have never been to Poland, know of the town of Częstochowa with its famous Paulite Monastery of Jasna Góra, if not from personal experience then at least from their parents. For centuries the Monastery at Jasna Góra has been one of the principal centres of religious life in Poland and the picture of Our Lady preserved there, hallowed by legend, has been the goal of pilgrimages for close on six centuries.

What many people do not know, however, is that the church and monastery at Jasna Góra are a treasury of national heirlooms, almost as important as the Wawel Cathedral in Cracow. There are various reasons for this. When in the last quarter of the 14th century Władysław Duke of Opole brought over a small group of Paulite Monks from Hungary and established them on top of a hill adjoining the village of Częstochowa, which was to become known as Jasna Góra, he probably never suspected the great future which awaited his modest foundation. At the time, the wooden church at Jasna Góra was already a centre of pilgrimages, but not as yet on a large scale. The goal of those pilgrimages was the Byzantine picture of Our Lady, which according to legend had been painted by St. Luke the Evangelist on a wooden plank which had served as a table-top in the house of the Holy Family at Nazareth.

The fame and renown of the Monastery spread enormously after the attack by Polish and Czech Hussite Brothers on Jasna Góra in 1430, during which they slashed the picture of the Madonna with swords. From that time on the Paulite Order at Jasna Góra came under the special protection of the kings of the Jagiellonian Dynasty, beginning with Władysław Jagiełło who conferred grants of land and privileges on the Monastery and ending with Sigismund the Old and his spouse, Bona Sforza, who endowed it with many priceless objects of worship of exceptional artistic value.

When the Reformation reached Poland in the 16th century the popularity of Jasna Góra somewhat diminished. But towards the end of that century when Catholicism gained a decisive victory in Poland and the Counter-Reformation ruled supreme, laying special emphasis on the cult of Mary, Jasna Góra returned to its former splendour and was again surrounded by very special royal protection. Sigismund III, Władysław IV and John Casimir of the Vasa Dynasty, and later King Michael Korybut Wiśniowiecki and John III Sobieski, always made a point of paying a visit to Częstochowa when journeying between Cracow and Warsaw. Each of those visits brought new gifts to the shrine. Sigismund III in particular, himself a skilled goldsmith, presented many valuable gifts of his own workmanship to the Monastery. Court painters and architects were commissioned to do work for the Monastery. It was to Władysław IV and his court architects that Jasna Góra Monastery owed its fortifications, which were to be put to such good use only a short time later.

In the mid-17th century Poland entered a difficult period of wars in the East, North and South. It began with the great Cossack Uprising under Bohdan Chmielnicki, followed by a Russian attack on the Grand Duchy of Lithuania and the Swedish invasion, most dangerous of all, supported by Brandenburg in the West and Hungary in the South. The Swedish "deluge" submerged the whole country: only Gdańsk and Lvov remained the lost islands of resistance; Lvov repulsed several enemy attacks. But both those cities were far from the centre of the country where towns and cities lacked proper fortification and could either put up no resistance or were forced to surrender after a short struggle. When Cracow fell and John Casimir was forced to seek refuge in Silesia, the Hetmans (military commanders) and their troops recognized the King of Sweden as their overlord and deep night seemed to have fallen over Poland.

It was then that an event occurred, which although of no great military significance, was to have incalculable consequences and bring about the country's awakening. In November 1655, a Swedish Army under General Müller began a siege of Jasna Góra, which was to last several weeks. The Monastery garrison put up a heroic defence which finally forced the Swedes to lift the siege and depart.

The brutality of Swedish troops had already resulted in partisan movements being organised here and there, mainly in Great Poland and in the mountainous south. Now, however, resistance spread throughout the country like wild fire. The attack on Jasna Góra was deemed an insult to the nation's religious feelings, and its successful defence was ascribed not so much to the courage of the garrison and strength of the defences, but to supernatural powers, in fact to the protection of the Holy Virgin to whom the shrine was dedicated. Contemporary literature played upon the nation's religious feelings and built a legend around the defence of Jasna Góra. On his return from exile John Casimir made a vow in Lvov Cathedral placing the country under the protection of Our Lady, and declared her Queen of the Crown of Poland. The Madonna's picture at Jasna Góra became the main symbol of her sovereignty over the country.

Once the Swedish "deluge" had been repulsed and peace with Sweden concluded, the Monastery at Jasna Góra became the goal of mass pilgrimages. Pilgrims coming to pray at the shrine of Our Lady would often bring votive gifts and thanksgiving offerings. The treasury at Jasna Góra was literally swamped with precious offerings, beginning with diadems, monstrances and chalices set in precious stones, and ending with modest votives wrought in silver. Hetmans offered up their *Bulawas* (the Hetman's staff of office), officers their commander's batons, knights their swords, armour and weapons taken from the enemy. Among the offerings is the sword of Hetman Żółkiewski, which the Paulite monks offered to John III Sobieski when on his way to relieve Vienna from the Turks. The King showed his gratitude by presenting the Monastery with trophies taken in the tents of the Grand Vizier Kara Mustafa. Other commanders serving under John III followed his example, so that within a short time the Monastery found itself in possession of a whole arsenal which required a special building to house it. With the passage of time legends grew round some of the most precious offerings. At the beginning of the 17th century the Paulite Monks drew up an inventory listing every item offered to the shrine, giving the date and name of the donor, for which we are indebted since these notes are today a source of historical importance.

By the second half of the 17th century the treasury at Jasna Góra was already a museum of artistic crafts. The collection kept growing with the centuries. In addition to examples of the gold and silversmith's art, it included tapestry, armour and weapons. The Monastery Church, the Chapel of Our Lady and monastery buildings were filled with mural paintings and pictures. Tomaso Dolabella of the Venetian school of painting and court painter to the King, considered the most outstanding artist in Poland at the time, worked at Jasna Góra in the early 17th century. The angels painted on the vaulted ceiling of the Chapel of Our Lady are undoubtedly his work and such paintings as "Holy Communion of the Jagiellonians" and "Our Lady Fighting off Heresy" carry the unmistakable stamp of his workshop. Dolabella delighted in painting historical subjects, large compositions crowded with figures. The Dolabella tradition, his method of composition, was continued at Jasna Góra up to the end of the 17th century by his pupils and his pupils' pupils. Unfortunately they have remained anonymous, but some of the artists may well have been members of the congregation, since every larger monastery in Poland at the time made it a point of having its own artists.

These later paintings display scenes from the history of the Paulite Order in Europe, in Poland and at Jasna Góra in particular. Outstanding among the many paintings is the "Siege of Jasna Góra by the Swedes" and the scene of the presentation of Żółkiewski's sword to John III Sobieski. Naturally, historical subjects are not the only ones to be admired at Jasna Góra. There are many pictures on a religious theme in the Church and Chapel of Our Lady, some of which represent considerable artistic value. A series of rectangular and oval coffin paintings, all connected with contemporary funeral ritual, are specially noteworthy. Fire destroyed the Church towards the end of the 17th century but fortunately the Chapel of Our Lady and Monastery escaped. After reconstruction, the Silesian painter Karl Dankwart covered the interior of the church with frescoes, mostly on Marian and symbolic themes, as well as scenes from the history of the Paulite Order.

There is also an exceptionally fine library in the Monastery, where many ancient books and manuscripts, rare or unique editions, Polish and foreign, have accumulated over the centuries. The library contains works published by the Paulite Fathers, for in fact the Monastery had its own printing works where books on various subjects apart from religious ones, were published. During the second half of the 17th century it published works of history and philosophy, amongst others by such outstanding writers as Wespazjan Kochowski and Stanisław Herakliusz Lubomirski. The library also possesses many rare illuminated manuscripts with hand-painted illustrations, some of which came from the Jagiellonian collections and were offered by members of the Dynasty.

The Paulite Fathers also possess richly endowed archives at Jasna Góra, which contain almost every document dealing with the history of the Order and of the Częstochowa Monastery in particular. There are also many documents of general national interest, autographed letters from the kings of Poland and letters from outstanding personalities who played a leading role in the country's political and cultural life. In sum the archives at Jasna Góra are a rich source of historical documentation of which Polish historians have not yet taken full advantage.

Fate was kind to the Jasna Góra collections. True, the fire at the close of the 17th century caused considerable losses and damage to the interior of the church. The final stormy period of Poland's independent existence also caused some loss, but the main core of the collection remained untouched. Following the loss of independence Jasna Góra Monastery found itself in the Russian partition where it was the only one not to be closed down by the Tsarist authorities. The Monastery survived both World Wars without suffering any significant damage. Having happily survived the many storms which fate did not spare the Polish nation, the Monastery at Jasna Góra remains an interesting architectural monument and a treasury of national heirlooms.

The Monastery collection was known to the public thanks to a printed guide to Jasna Góra. Part of the treasury was also open to the public, but no scientifically prepared inventory existed. In recent years the Institute of Art of the Polish Academy of Sciences by agreement with the Church authorities, began drawing up a systematic inventory of the treasures at Jasna Góra.

Art historians, Zofia Rozanow and Ewa Smulikowska, authors of this work, drew up an inventory on behalf of the Institute. Hence this is a first-hand publication, coming from the pens of the two most competent persons whose great merit it is to have compiled an exhaustive inventory of the wealth and variety of the treasures at Jasna Góra.

The results of cataloguing works of art throughout the whole country are being published in serial form under the general title of "Catalogue of Works of Art in Poland". A separate volume of the publication is devoted to each voivodship and contains chapters on individual counties. The work is continuing according to an overall plan. It is hoped that the results of the cataloguing at Jasna Góra will shortly be published, and that as Volume XVI of the Art Catalogue they will form part of the special series on great cities and places of exceptional interest, such as the Royal Castle of Wawel.

Before this strictly professional publication is printed, the authors of the present work are sharing the results of their meritorious work with the public. Hence this is not a work destined for specialists only, and it should arouse the interest of everybody to whom Polish culture is not a matter of indifference. In easy and accessible style, the authors provide an outline of the history of the Monastery at Jasna Góra and then give information on the most interesting historical heirlooms and works of art accumulated over the centuries in the Monastery collection.

This work is intended for both Polish and foreign readers, but above all for the large numbers of Polish emigrants scattered throughout the world, for whom recollections of their Fatherland remain alive and close to their hearts.

I have no doubt that this well written work on the *Cultural Heritage of Jasna Góra* will arouse lively interest.

Władysław Tomkiewicz

Contents

THE CULTURAL HERITAGE
OF JASNA GÓRA

VERYBODY in Poland has heard of Częstochowa but very few people know its extremely interesting history. Here, probably more than in any other place in Poland, a splendid and extremely varied collection has accumulated over the last six centuries, testifying to the profound patriotism of the Polish people, their ties with the national culture and national tradition. The Monastery at Jasna Góra is a unique national monument which escaped the plunder and looting which accompanied many national disasters. Ever since its foundation in 1382, Jasna Góra has been closely tied with Polish national history, as proved by the numerous national heirlooms which have accumulated there. At the time of its foundation there was nothing to point to the role the Paulite Monastery was to play in Polish history. Circumstances in which the foundation was made are well known today. It was proclaimed by Louis of Anjou, King of Poland and Hungary, already on his death-bed, who sent Władysław Duke of Opole, his Palatine and nephew to perform the act of foundation. The foundation was located on a spot which had been inhabited for centuries. Częstochowa Hill is the culminating height of the Cracow-Częstochowa Jura hence it may be supposed that it was there that the earliest signs of settle-

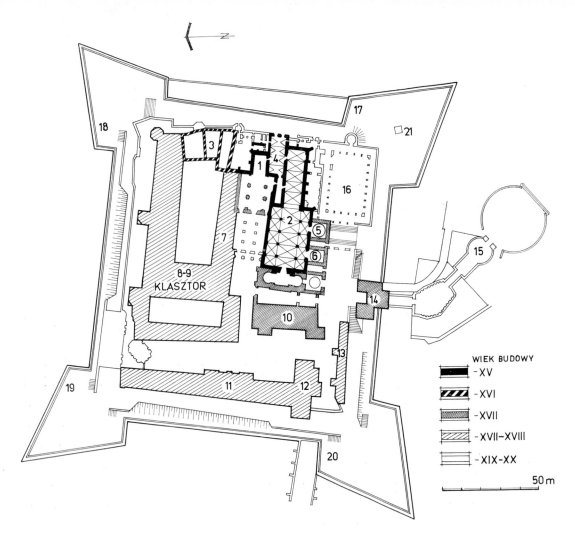

Explanations to the Plan of Jasna Góra

1. Chapel of Our Lady ; 2. Church of the Assumption ; 3. The Monastery, former Abbots' houses ; 4. The Sacristy ; 5. Jabłonowski Family Chapel ; 6. Denhoff Family Chapel ; 7. The Monastery, Knights' Hall (First floor) ; 8. The Monastery, Refectory (Ground floor) ; 9. The Monastery Library (First floor) ; 10. Royal Apartments ; 11. Printing House ; 12. Arsenal ; 13. Musicians' Houses ; 14. Jagiellonian Gate ; 15. Lubomirski Gate ; 16. Chapel of the Last Supper ; 17. Potocki Bastion ; 18. Szaniawski Bastion ; 19. Morsztyn Bastion ; 20. Lubomirski Bastion ; 21. Statue of Father Augustyn Kordecki.

ment were to be found. It may be surmised that in the 12th and 13th centuries, a small fortified place and a chapel or modest little church existed there.

When the Paulite Fathers took possession of Jasna Góra in June 1382 a wooden church dedicated to Our Lady, Virgin and Mother, was already in existence. The parish priest who handed the church over to the Paulite Monks was Henryk Biel of Błeszno, who bore the Ostoja coat-of-arms. The first monks, numbering about twelve, came from the Church of St. Lawrence near Buda in Hungary, where the Order had a richly endowed monastery.

The act of foundation performed by Duke Władysław was nominal rather than practical, since the endowment consisted of rents which were hard to exact in the sparsely populated region of Częstochowa. Hence it may be surmised that during their first years at Jasna Góra, the Paulite Monks could not afford any major construction work.

After the death of King Louis, the political career of the Duke of Opole came to a rapid end. Power was taken over by the great lords of Little Poland, who set their heart on marrying off Jadwiga, daughter of Louis of Hungary, to the Grand Duke of Lithuania, Władysław Jagiełło. Jagiełło re-endowed the monastery and in 1393 granted it new privileges which established material conditions for the monastery's development. Queen Jadwiga contributed to the re-endowment of Jasna Góra. The royal document states plainly that the endowment was made by the King and his beloved Queen, Jadwiga.

It may be taken that the King linked his dynastic plans with the Paulite Order, emphasising his zeal as a convert, which strengthened his position, in face of the hostile policy of the Habsburgs. The Habsburgs refused to recognize the legality of the wedding between Jadwiga and Jagiełło because it had frustrated their own dynastic plans. They spread the argument throughout all the courts of Europe, that the marriage was illegal, in view of the betrothal ceremony celebrated in childhood between Jadwiga and William of Habsburg and also because the husband of that Christian Queen was a pagan. Hence in his relations with the Roman-Catholic Church, Jagiełło always emphasised his zeal as a Catholic, confirming it by numerous church endowments.

VLADISLAVS
DVX OPOLIENSIS
A SCITHICA INCVR-
SIONE OPE ODYGITRIAE.
VIRGINIS LIBER ET VICTOR
IN ARCE BELSENSI EVADENS.
FRATRES ORD: S. PAVLI PRIMI
EREM: DIVINITVS PRAEMONSTRA-
TOS, EX HVNGARIA VOCATOS
IN MONTEM CLARVM. TRADITO
ILLIS SACRO THEOTOCO INTRO-
DVCIT, ET BENIGNISSIME FVN-
DAT ECCLESIA PAROCHIALI
MVTATA IN RELIGIOSAM,
COLLATIS ET NONNVLLIS
DECIMIS ET FVNDIS
ANNO
1382.

Foundation of Jasna Góra Monastery in 1382; Władysław Duke of Opole placing the picture of Our Lady in the care of the Paulite Monks; a picture from the cycle of paintings showing the history of Jasna Góra; 2nd half of the 17th century. Knights' Hall

Foundation of Jasna Góra Monastery in 1382; Jasna Góra School, circa 1630. The Arsenal

LADISLAVS DVX OPPOLIEŃ FRATRES ORDIN.S. PAVLI PRI MI EREMITÆ IN EC CLESIAM CLARO MONTANAM IN

The turning point in the history of Jasna Góra was the appearance of the picture of Our Lady.

The opinion prevails that the picture of Our Lady was transferred to Jasna Góra in 1384, two years after the act of foundation performed by the Duke of Opole. Careful study of recently discovered documents disclosed that the Duke of Opole acquired the picture in Ruthenia where it was surrounded with great reverence and worshipped as a priceless relic, connected with the life of the Holy Family. True to Byzantine tradition, it was richly ornamented in gold and jewels of great value. Legend holds that the Duke first saw the picture at Belz Castle and at once conceived the plan of removing it to Opole. It is not known what circumstances decided that it was ultimately left at Jasna Góra. Tradition holds this was due to miraculous intervention. A comparison of dates brings us to the conclusion that the Duke banished to Opole by King Władysław Jagiełło was carrying away his booty from Ruthenia. The booty was considerable and in addition to the picture of the Madonna, included other magnificent icons studded with gold and precious stones. It may well be that fearing to lose his treasure and hoping to keep at least part of it for himself, he left the picture of Our Lady at Jasna Góra, where it was to remain. The picture brought great changes to the role played by the first Paulite Monastery in Poland. Originally the Paulite Fathers were a reclusive penitent order. Their monastic rule orders seclusion, long periods of contemplation, hours of silence and doing severe penance. It is an order which abhors contact with the outside world. But the presence of the picture, within a few years made Częstochowa one of the greatest and best known centres of pilgrimage, not only in Poland but in the whole of Central Europe. The famous historian Jan Długosz wrote of Jasna Góra that it had become the goal of pilgrimages from Silesia, Moravia, Hungary and Prussia. The growing cult of Our Lady of Częstochowa rapidly made the Monastery a rich and flourishing centre of pilgrimage.

Jan Długosz makes repeated mention of the Paulite Monastery each time giving a somewhat altered version. He repeats the legend according to which the picture of Our Lady was to have been painted by St. Luke the Evangelist,

The miraculous picture of Our
Lady of Częstochowa

another time that it was painted in strange and unusual fashion, the eyes following the viewer in every direction. He also mentions it installed in the new church, and says he could remember it in the old, wooden church. There is nothing strange in that; Długosz was born in Brzeźnica near Częstochowa and was fifteen years old at the time of the foundation of the new church. So of course he could remember the little old church on the top of Częstochowa Hill, where the picture was preserved at first.

A sad event of great importance in the history of the Paulite Monastery occurred in 1430. It was sacrilegiously attacked during Holy Week that year. The picture of Our Lady was seized from the high-altar, profaned and terribly damaged, with sabre slashes and sword thrusts. Hussites from across the Bohemian and Moravian border led by the Volhynian prince Fedor Ostrogski were responsible for the crime. It had every appearance of an attempt being motivated by religious hatred, but it must not be forgotten that it also had a political background, for the Volhynian prince entertained close relations with Witold, Grand Duke of Lithuania and later with his successor Swidrygiełło, both of whom were at odds with Jagiełło as to the future of the Lithuanian crown. Hence there is some reason to suspect that the real motive behind the crime was to stir up political trouble. Długosz tells that when suspicion fell on Silesian and Czech Hussites, Jagiełło came within an inch of taking military measures. Two of the culprits were apprehended and executed at the Royal Castle in Cracow. Both were members of the Polish nobility.

The picture, in seriously damaged condition, was taken to Cracow, where it was restored with a care and devotion unprecedented in medieval Poland.

According to the prevailing custom and in conformance with the demands of Catholic liturgy, holy pictures or statues which had suffered profanation were displayed in church where a solemn service beseeching God's pardon was said over them. They were washed in holy water and penitential prayers were recited. Only after all those rites and ceremonies had been completed could they be restored to their former place.

But we learn from contemporary sources that the picture of Our Lady was displayed in the Cracow Town Hall, and placed in the care of the Council.

Face of the Blessed Virgin Mary, detail from the picture of Our Lady

23

There it underwent restoration. An interesting piece of information has come to light in connection with this. It seems that the reason why the picture was left in the Town Hall was because it was decided to institute court proceedings against the parties guilty of the sacrilege. The picture was to testify against them. The painting had been very seriously damaged, and the circumstances of its restoration are mysterious. Contemporary sources tell that Ruthenian painters employed at the Court were the first to try their skill in restoring it. They made three efforts all without success, each time the paints would run. The cuts and bruises refused to take paint — a contemporary report by Risinius (Piotr of Rozprza) said. Jagiełło dismissed them and sent for artists of the Imperial Habsburg Court, who were probably of Czech origin. They were told to bring credentials testifying to their proficiency. They set to work laughing at the lack of ability of their predecessors, but twice over their own efforts proved unsuccessful. The third time however they did succeed and the painting was finally restored — so the legend goes. King Jagiełło provided new wrought gold ornamental sheeting for the picture. It was then returned to Częstochowa and installed over the high-altar in the Chapel of Our Lady. All this sounded like a typical medieval saga.

It has to be stated, however, that as a work of art the picture of Our Lady of Częstochowa despite two thorough examinations by conservation experts, still contains elements of mystery.

The first restoration was carried out in 1925—26 by Professor Jan Rutkowski (head of the painting conservation of the State Art Collections in Warsaw). According to Prof. Rutkowski, the original painting damaged during the attack in 1430, restored and repainted, has been preserved until today. On the basis of the 1926 findings, the picture's stylistic affinities were traced to the Italian painting of the 12th—14th centuries, and its appearance at Jasna Góra linked to the Angevin dynasty. (This view was held by W. Podlacha, S. Tomkowicz and K. Pieradzka). K. Estreicher, however, ascribed the picture to Bohemian painting of about 1350. In 1971 E. Śnieżyńska-Stolot reverting to the theory of the Hungarian provenance of the painting attributed it to the Italian circle of Simone-Martini which arose in the first quarter of the 14th century.

The Hussite attack in 1430. Profanation and destruction of the picture of Our Lady (fragment); from the cycle illustrating the history of Jasna Góra. End of the 17th century. Knights' Hall

A second restoration was carried out in 1948—52 by Professor Rudolf Kozłowski (conservator of the department of painting of the State Wawel Collections). According to Prof. Kozłowski the present picture is a homogeneous work executed in its entirety after 1430. It replaced the considerably older original painting of which only the boards on which it was painted have been preserved, and the rare and untypical representation of Our Lady of Częstochowa can be explained by the fact that it was copied from the previous picture. The microscopic fragment of canvas under the present picture, originating, according to Prof. Kozłowski, from the original painting, has a glue finish, which suggests that the original painting might have been executed by the wax technique. This would indicate a much earlier origin of the first picture. As a result of research carried out by Prof. Kozłowski the assumption that the Częstochowa picture is of oriental origin and was possibly executed by a method not used in the West, became more possible. M. Walicki believed that the original painting was based on a Byzantine model, but at the time of its destruction in 1430 it consisted of several layers and repainted sections, most of its features being typical of the 14th century Angevin circle. On the other hand T. Mroczko and B. Dąb assume that the original painting was an oriental icon which, because of its composition and the presence of halos in relief could not originate earlier than the 13th century.

Thus after the two restorations and thorough expert examinations of the picture carried out at an interval of 25 years the basic question remains: Italian or Byzantine-Kievan? An original 13th—14th century painting or a work done in Cracow after 1430? A gift of the Angevin dynasty or a Ruthenian trophy of Władysław of Opole? The above divergences of opinion show conclusively that the period of research is only beginning and the technical methods perfected over the last 20 years may bring an explanation of the complex problem of the history of the Częstochowa Madonna.

If, however, we were to accept Prof. Kozłowski's hypothesis that the first picture was executed by the encaustic technique, the traditional legend about the difficulties in restoring the damaged picture could be explained. Obviously, tempera paints used during attempts at restoration in 1434 would not hold on the wax paints. The work performed by the anonymous Imperial court-painters after several unsuccessful attempts, was indeed quite exceptional.

Since the original painting resisted all efforts at restoration, they made a faithful copy of it, with the greatest attention to detail, after which what was left of the original silk canvas with the wax paint was scraped off and the board planed down and reinforced with a large, thick framework. The copy of the original painting was then fitted back on the original board. To perpetuate the memory of the sacrilegious attempt two cuts were scored on the right cheek of Our Lady's face and filled with red paint. The question arises, why was the picture of Our Lady of Częstochowa treated in such an unusual manner? Why were such painstaking efforts made to preserve the original board, when it would have been much easier to provide a new one?

It must be remembered that the Częstochowa picture played a very special role in the cult of Mary. It was not just a painting of Our Lady, but according to tradition, a relic connected with her life on earth. Legend holds it was painted on a board which had been the table-top at which the Holy Family in Nazareth used to work and take their meals. During the Middle Ages, objects in any way connected with the life of Jesus and His Holy Mother were considered as relics of the highest order. The table-board from Nazareth was one of the most venerated relics in Christian Europe. The exceptional trouble taken during the work of restoration was intended to preserve this relic connected with the life of Our Lady. The painting itself was copied with the most meticulous care. All this was at the origin of the picture's most unusual aspect, which painted in the 1430s, combines ancient-Christian and Byzantine characteristics with a 14th century style of painting. It is executed in so-called soft technique by an outstanding contemporary artist (or artists) who succeeded in creating a wonderfully harmonious and extremely suggestive work of art of the highest quality. Quite apart from its importance as an object of the cult, the picture of Our Lady of Częstochowa is a magnificent example of the Gothic school of painting in Poland. Probably on the occasion of its restoration under Jagiełło, the picture was given triptych form. The two closing wings were painted with the likenesses of St. Catherine and St. Barbara. The fame of its restora-

tion in mysterious circumstances and the devotion displayed by Jagiełło, made Jasna Góra one of the best known centres of pilgrimage. The original Late-Gothic chapel was given a star-vaulted ceiling at the beginning of the 16th century and became the presbytery. After 1609 the original mural paintings were covered over with Late-Renaissance Italian-style frescoes, probably the work of the court-painter Tomaso Dolabella, of Venice. The eight angel figures painted on the vaulting carry the unmistakable characteristics of his brush and two large mural paintings on the side-walls, representing the Presentation of Our Lord in the Temple and the Adoration of the Virgin Mary and Child Jesus by St. Catherine and St. Barbara are also ascribed to him.

All that is left of the original Gothic décor of the Chapel of Our Lady is a monumental crucifix, which was moved to the side-altar on the right in 1659. Recent studies proved it is of late 15th century workmanship. Some of its characteristics place it among outstanding works of the Cracow School from the circle of Wit Stwosz, one of the greatest European sculptors.

The setting round the picture was also changed. After 1600 the original Gothic triptych was replaced by a Late-Renaissance gilded altar retable. Its aspect has been handed down to us with considerable fidelity in the painting representing the "Communion of the Jagiellonians," also the work of Dolabella. Soon however, this retable was considered too modest for the picture, which was surrounded with constantly growing veneration. In 1650, Jerzy Ossoliński, Grand Chancellor of the Crown, endowed the chapel with a magnificent altar-piece, which is to be seen in the chapel presbytery to this day. This altar is considered one of the best examples of 17th century Baroque in Poland. Of wooden construction, it is lined in ebony veneer. Magnificent silver ornaments executed by the famous Pomeranian goldsmith Christian Bierpfaff, who worked in Toruń and Gdańsk, contrast beautifully with the distinguished black of the ebony. The miraculous picture, set high above the crowds of worshippers, was the object of constantly growing veneration, as a national relic, but ornaments which kept being added, tended to obscure the view. Between 1641 and 1644 a massive grill of Gdańsk workmanship founded by primate Maciej Łubieński was added separating the

The Chapel of Our Lady: late-Gothic vaulted ceiling in the Presbytery

Late-Gothic crucifix; circle of Wit
Stwosz, Cracow School, late 15th
century. Chapel of Our Lady, side-
altar on the right

Late-Gothic crucifix, Head of Christ

The Chapel of Our Lady: evening service before the picture. View of the Presbytery and altar founded by Chancellor Jerzy Ossoliński in 1650

Silver figure of kneeling angel, fragment of the old tabernaculum from the altar in the Chapel of Our Lady, by the Toruń goldsmith Jan Chrystian Bierpfaff executed in 1650. Treasury

33

picture from the enlarged nave of the chapel. In 1673 a magnificent silver covering in repoussé workmanship was made for the picture. A votive offering of the Działyński family, the cover represented the dogma of the Immaculate Conception, of the work of Jan Loman. To this day it is ceremoniously raised to the sound of fanfares, usually during religious services only.

The ultimate decorative element which came to add splendour to the retable was a great silver antependium, specially made for the coronation of the miraculous picture in 1717. The central part presents a contemporary view of Jasna Góra, as a symbolic stronghold of Divine Power. The custom of adorning the picture with ornamental jewelled robes, made of the precious stones which flowed in as votive offerings, originated in the 17th century or strictly speaking, in its latter half. The robes are preserved to this day. They represent a unique, spontaneous collection of which there will be further mention later in this work. As concerns architecture, Jasna Góra represents a sum total of the tastes of several periods: for example its Gothic centre combines harmoniously with additions and conversions of the Baroque period.

Late-Baroque ornaments in the interior of the Basilica, the 17th and 18th century architectural groups added at Jasna Góra, have retained their pure, unblemished original form. Hence they are of quite exceptional value to the history of art in Poland. This group of buildings, almost unique of its kind, possesses complete archive documentation of every work of art which exists there and is more closely connected with the national saga and history than any other place in Poland, with the possible exception of Wawel and the Royal Castle in Warsaw.

Only thirty years after it was built, the small original church, destined for the exclusive use of the Paulite monks, could no longer hold the flocking crowds of the faithful. Construction of a vast new church began in the 'sixties of the 15th century. It was given three large naves equal in elevation, typical of a pilgrimage shrine. It stands to this day, but after the fire in 1690, was converted to a basilica, the central nave being raised.

Additions were gradually built round the 15th century Gothic central part. Originally they formed a compact, enclosed group of buildings, consisting of

Antependium of the Chapel of Our
Lady altar. Repoussé silver showing
the fortress of Jasna Góra, circa 1717

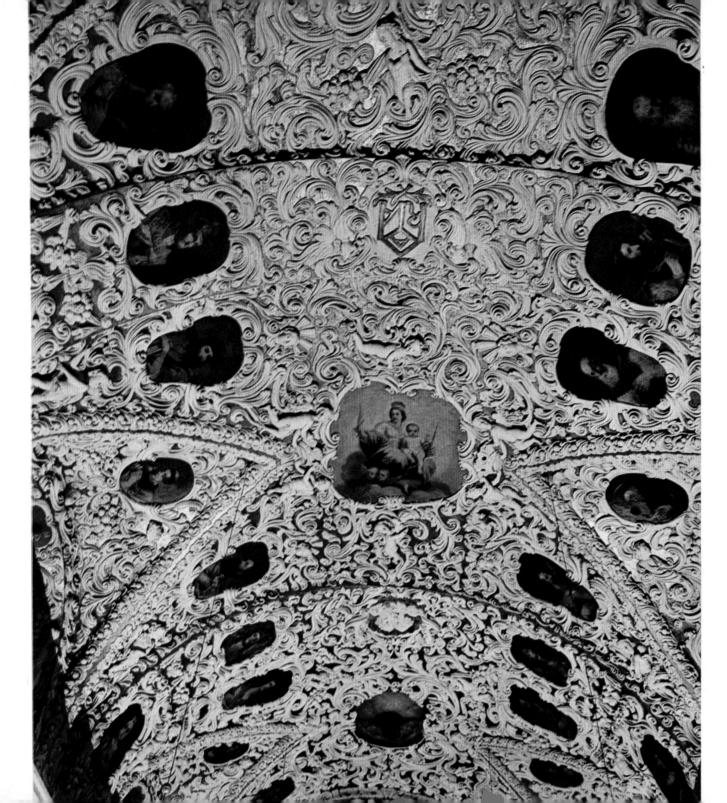

The Chapel of Our Lady, ceiling in the nave, showing 17th century stucco work

The Chapel of Our Lady, view of the north gallery from the south gallery. Interior of the nave in Lublin-Kalisz style, 1644

the church, the Chapel of Our Lady and the monastery quadrangle. Reports of the visitation by Cardinal Jerzy Radziwiłł in 1593 disclose that the church and monastery buildings were Gothic. The Cardinal noted the urgent need for improvements that existed. One was to enlarge the Chapel of Our Lady which could no longer contain the crowds of faithful flocking to worship the miraculous picture. This presented many difficulties because the chapel could only be extended in the westernly direction, where the original monastery quadrangle stood. Contemporary sources tell that in accordance with ancient practice they were built of hewn stone, very solid and durable. In all probability the quandrangle was in Gothic style and had a central arched courtyard. In its place the three-nave extension to the chapel was built in 1644, just as it stands today. It should be stressed that this is an outstanding example of Lublin-style architecture, typical in Poland between the Mannerism and Baroque periods. The noble proportions of individual items of architecture, the beautiful stucco ornaments, completed only in the 'eighties of the 17th century, on the vaults and ceiling of the central nave, the fine sculptures in marble and alabaster, make the Chapel of Our Lady one of the best examples of Polish architecture of the Counter-Reformation period.

The next work of construction undertaken at Jasna Góra by King Sigismund III, was on the defences. Defences raised in that King's reign consisted of earthworks with four bastions only but a first bastion facing the town was also raised. The next stage was in the reigns of Władysław IV and John Casimir. The Monastery was surrounded by a rectangle of defence walls with bastions jutting out in front. This system of fortifications known as new-Italo-Dutch, was generally established in Europe after the invention of fire-arms. Jasna Góra was turned into one of the more important strongholds in Poland and successfully withstood siege by a Swedish army in 1655.

Nevertheless in view of the constant development of military techniques, the fortifications of Jasna Góra in the second half of the century required enlarging and strengthening. Already in 1657 during their stay in Jasna Góra, king John Casimir and his wife Maria Louise set an example by taking part in the raising

Jasna Góra. East view of the Monastery

40

The Denhoff Chapel: domed ceiling. Frescoes with scenes from the life of St. Paul the Hermit and St. Anthony. Stucco work by Franciszek Zaor, executed in 1671

The Denhoff Chapel: grating in the entrance with the Paulite Arms, circa 1670

of earthworks. In 1674 thanks to the generosity of the starosta (king's governor) of Oświęcim Jan Odrowąż Pieniążek, a royal architect Krzysztof Mieroszewski was commissioned to design the reconstruction of a south-east bastion of the stronghold. In 1676 in front of the walls an independent minor fortification was set up. It was to protect the south-east and south-west bastions as well as the main entrance to the stronghold.

In the first half of the 18th century, according to the new requirements of strategy a complete modernisation of the stronghold was carried out. The whole system of fortifications was surrounded with a widened moat and palisade. South-east and west bastions were expanded in 1742—1745 after the designs of the engineer Krystian Dahlke. In 1750 both bastions were rebuilt from the north-east and west, while all the walls were given a brick facing. At the time of the Bar Confederacy, in 1770 when the importance of the Jasna Góra stronghold was again to prove vital, Casimir Pułaski leading the defence ordered a fortified camp to be set up and strengthened with additional entrenchments, which took up the entire summit of Częstochowa hill.

Between the First and Second Partitions of Poland, plans were made to reinforce the defences at Jasna Góra, but they were never put into execution. Nevertheless Jasna Góra must still have been a powerful stronghold since it withstood attacks by Austrian troops in 1809, during the Duchy of Warsaw period. Tsar Alexander I was also aware of the military importance of Jasna Góra and of its symbolic significance to the Polish nation. After the fall of the Duchy of Warsaw in 1813 and the occupation of Częstochowa by Russian troops he ordered the defences of the fortress to be pulled down. The walls, bastions and earthworks were destroyed, and only the gates leading into the Monastery were left intact. This state of things lasted only thirty years in all. In 1843 Tsar Nicholas I ordered the defences rebuilt. The defences were rebuilt with locally quarried stone and given a brick facing. The reason for this apparently surprising decision was the Tsar's wish to demonstrate his tolerance and good-will towards the Church, in the eyes of all Europe.

In addition to the fortifications, other work of construction was also continued. A multi-storey tower was built over the western church elevation

View of the gates and approaches seen from the steeple

42

View of the south wing of the Monastery from the steeple showing the Chapel of Our Lady and Basilica

Jasna Góra. The Basilica, view of the series of domed porches, side chapels and belfry. The Arsenal is seen in the foreground on the left and the Musicians' House on the right

between 1620 and 1630 to which a monumental, domed porch of noble proportions, in the style of a Renaissance chapel, was added on the south side. Very probably it was also used as a stage, where occasional religious plays were given.

A row of three domed edifices was built along the southern side of the church in the 17th century, probably in imitation of the chapels along the southern wall of Wawel Cathedral.

The second and finest of the three, the sepulchral chapel of the Denhoff family, is one of the best examples of the so-called Vasa-Baroque period in Poland. Built between 1644 and 1671, it has stucco ornaments by the Cracow artist Franciszek Zaor. It has been preserved in perfect condition to this day.

The double chapel of the Holy Relics and the Holy Guardian Angels is the third of the domed edifices, counting from the presbytery end. Its lower floor contains relics of several saints, the upper is the mausoleum of the Jabłonowski family. It was erected in two stages. The first chapel founded by the Paulite provincial Mikołaj Królik was erected in 1625 as a chapel to house the relics of the Holy Martyrs which had been brought from Rome. In 1751—1754 it was completely rebuilt and its upper floor, known ever since as the Holy Guardian Angels' or the Jabłonowski chapel, was now to serve as a mausoleum of one of the order's benefactors, Stanisław Jabłonowski, voivode of Rawa. Relics of Martyrs were housed from then on in the cellars of the converted chapel traditionally known as the chapel of Holy Relics.

The Monastery at Jasna Góra built over a period of two centuries is a mighty, rectangular block of buildings rising to three storeys. The two wings are occupied by the monks' cells, the central part contains representative apartments.

The first floor of the southern wing, above the Rosary Chapel, is occupied by the Knights' Hall, rising to a height of two storeys. It was built in 1649 not only for monastic ceremonies but with a thought to public occasions also. Sessions of the Senate of the Realm were sometimes held there. The marriage between King Michael Korybut Wiśniowiecki and Eleonora, Archduchess of Austria was celebrated in the west wing in 1670. The new refectory was hastily

Mementoes of Poles imprisoned in
concentration camps during the Second World War. Treasury

The Refectory: Ceiling frescoes. The centre part with a wedding wreath was painted for the wedding ceremony of king Michael Korybut Wiśniowiecki

The Refectory. Interior completed in 1670. Ceiling frescoes by Karl Dankwart completed after 1690

completed for the occasion. Numerous gifts offered then by the royal couple and guests present at the wedding ceremonies are preserved in the Monastery treasury.

Although in the course of the 600 years of Jasna Góra's existence historical defeats happily passed the monastery by, it nevertheless succumbed to disaster at the hands of the elements when, in 1690, both the church and the monastery were consumed by fire.

News of the fire at Jasna Góra, a place already dear to the heart of every Pole, re-echoed loudly throughout the country. Great nobles and people of humble origin all declared readiness to contribute to the reconstruction. A letter from King John III Sobieski, expressing his dismay at the news that the shrine had been damaged by fire and promising a large sum of money for its reconstruction, is preserved in the Monastery archives. A letter from the poet Wespazjan Kochowski is another interesting document. Suffering from a heavy sickness, he was unable to come in person " to serve with consolation" but declared he was writing a poem he named *Rubus Incombustus* (The Burning Bush) and dedicated to Jasna Góra.

Thanks to the generosity of many people, the damage was rapidly repaired. Paintings on the new ceiling of the Basilica were completed in 1693. The well-known painter Karl Dankwart completed the frescoes in under three years. Some of the frescoes in the refectory and Monastery sacristy are also his work. The great work of reconstruction carried out after the fire at Jasna Góra was initiated by the Prior, Father Tobiasz Czechowicz, and continued by Father Konstanty Moszyński, prior and provincial, well-known patron of the arts. During his frequent visits in Rome, he had fallen under the spell of Italian art. It is above all to him that the Basilica at Jasna Góra owes its conversion and decorations in Late Baroque style. The high altar and side altars in painted, gilt and imitation marble stucco are among the best examples of early 18th century art in Poland. In the 18th century other buildings intended to serve various purposes were added. The existing arsenal was enlarged to meet the essential needs of defence. A printing-house was built and

Knights' Hall, general view of the interior (1647). Since 1660 occasionally used for sessions of the Polish Senate

50

remained in operation for two centuries. Many valuable books were printed there, by no means of a religious nature only.

The monks also built so-called musicians' houses, to house lay musicians of the Jasna Góra orchestra and their families.

Closed within the confines of the stronghold the characteristic architectural shape of the Jasna Góra complex has not basically undergone any major transformations since the end of the 18th century.

During the difficult post-partition period Jasna Góra became a symbol binding together the three parts of the dismembered country, upholding the patriotic traditions which the partitioning powers endeavoured to suppress. Jasna Góra became a holy national shrine in the eyes of the whole Polish nation, where apart from priceless works of art, historical relics and mementoes loaded with great emotional significance for a nation deprived of its freedom, were preserved.

This significance of Jasna Góra gained prominence once more during the dark period of Nazi occupation. Heart-rending mementoes from concentration camps and votive offerings from Polish soldiers who fought on every front in the Second World War, have found a worthy place in the Treasury at Jasna Góra.

Several works of restoration were undertaken at Jasna Góra during the 19th century but no construction work of any greater significance. The statue of Father Kordecki, by the Warsaw sculptor Henryk Statler, was erected on the fortress battlements in 1859, to remind the nation that in times of stress faith in ultimate victory must never be abandoned. In reprisal for the national uprising of 1863, the tsarist authorities confiscated all remaining monastery property. A statue of Tsar Alexander II was erected in the square on the eastern side of the hill, just below the Monastery. After the First World War it was pulled down and replaced by a statue of the Holy Virgin Mary.

The end of the 19th and beginning of the 20th century saw a revival of construction work. In 1891 a new gate crowned by a stone statue of the Sorrowful Mother of God was erected on the site of the old one which had gone

Siege of Jasna Góra by the Swedes in 1655; fragment from the picture of Father Kordecki

Father Augustyn Kordecki, (d. 1672). View from the window in the background shows the siege of Jasna Góra by the Swedes in 1655. Knights' Hall

A.R.P. AUGUSTINUS KORDECKI
TER PROVINCIALIS POL. PLUS O
RANDI QUAM PRÆLIANDI GNARUS, BEL
LUM TAMEN UTI PRIOR CLAROMON
TANUS CUM 12 MILLIBVS SVECORUM
IN HOC SACRO MONTE PRO FIDE
ET PATRIA SVSCEPIT ET GLORIOS
SSIME ABEGIT 1655 INCVIUS PRÆMI
UM INFULA A SERENISSIMO IOAN
NE CASIMIRO REGALE DECUSAT
ILLAM, INNATA HUMILITATE SPRE
VIT, UT CORONAM GLORIÆ MERE
RETUR IN COELIS, PRO QUA A.

to ruin. A second bridge, made necessary by the constantly growing crowds of pilgrims flocking to the shrine, was built alongside the existing one, connecting outer fortifications with the inner Monastery.

In 1900 the steeple of Jasna Góra Church was destroyed by fire. It was rebuilt between 1900 and 1906, according to plans by the well-known architects Stefan Szyller and Józef Dziekoński.

In 1903 a new apex was added to the Chapel of Our Lady, and an altar in the outer gallery where, in conformance with 17th century tradition, services were held during special ceremonies.

Between 1900 and 1913 Stations of the Cross were erected outside the defence walls. The work of the sculptor Pius Weloński, they were set up on monumental stone pedestals designed by the already mentioned Stefan Szyller. The last two works of construction at Jasna Góra were carried out during the inter-war period. One was the Confession House and the other is the Chapel of the Last Supper, a rectangular gallery and chapel, where pilgrims' confessions are heard and Holy Communion given. Both buildings were built between 1921 and 1927, to a design by the architect Adolf Szyszko-Bohusz. The bas-relief sculpture on the Chapel front is considered one of the best works by the sculptor Tadeusz Hukan.

*

Jasna Góra has been the site of many memorable events closely connected with Polish history. We shall mention only the most important ones.

During the Swedish "deluge" the Monastery at Jasna Góra experienced difficult moments. No great damage or destruction was caused, but the threat to the Monastery, the people who had sought refuge there and to the treasures of art it contained had been very real indeed. The Swedish attack on the

Siege of Jasna Góra by the Swedes in 1655. Painted 1656—1657; the Chapel of Our Lady

Siege of Jasna Góra by the Swedes in 1655. Detail of a picture from the cycle on the history of Jasna Góra. End of the 17th century. Knights' Hall

Detail of the picture showing the great fire of Jasna Góra in 1690, from the cycle on the history of Jasna Góra, painted after 1690. Knights' Hall

The Basilica; view of the nave and presbytery ceiling. Ceiling polychrome by Karl Dankwart painted in 1693. Marble-imitation painting on walls executed between 1770 and 1780

The Basilica; ceiling of the south aisle with non-painted keystone; polychrome by Karl Dankwart, executed in 1693

shrine was a great shock to the whole Polish nation and was to remain in its memory a long time. It must be remembered that the Swedes captured and destroyed all the more important centres of resistance in the country, including the most fortified strongholds. If they failed to gain entry by force of arms, they would achieve their purpose with the help of bribery.

Jasna Góra was one of the few fortified places which never fell to them. In 1655 its fortifications were strong and capable of holding out against a siege. It had a strong garrison, all necessary supplies and a source of water within the walls, which exists to this day. The Monks received advance information of the approach of the Swedish army.

Foreseeing a lengthy siege, Father Kordecki's first step was to reinforce the garrison and organise a relief force. Members of the congregation were sent as emissaries to Silesia, the Cracow area and the mountainous region of the Carpathians. Supplied with large sums of money from the Monastery treasury they formed units composed of mercenary troops, which were to operate in the enemy rear. At the same time new weapons were purchased for the Monastery garrison and large supplies of gun-powder were brought in. When the Swedish army under General Müller hove in sight, the defenders were in a position to refuse any offer of surrender. The Swedes had great expectations of capturing the Monastery treasury. They had looted many churches and knew what riches were to be found. It must be remembered they looted the treasury of nearly every more important church in Poland. Archives of the Cathedral in Gniezno contain reports of Cathedral Canons tortured and scorched with red-hot irons to extract information as to where the cathedral gold and silver had been buried. Every time Müller demanded the gates be opened to him, Father Kordecki, mindful of the relief force which was being organised, endeavoured to extend negotiations, writing diplomatically worded replies. Each time the Swedes thought they were within sight of success, operations organised by the Monks in their rear forced them to a change of plans. Finally the Swedes raised the siege just before Christmas which was celebrated in complete freedom.

The Basilica; view of the Nave and Presbytery

The Basilica; High Altar (1726) —
centre group shows the Virgin Mary
supported by angels. View from a-
bove

The Basilica; south aisle. Altar on
"rainbow" wall: 1. St. Anne, circa
1730; 2. St. Luke, second half of
the 18th century and the picture of
St. Joseph, 17th century

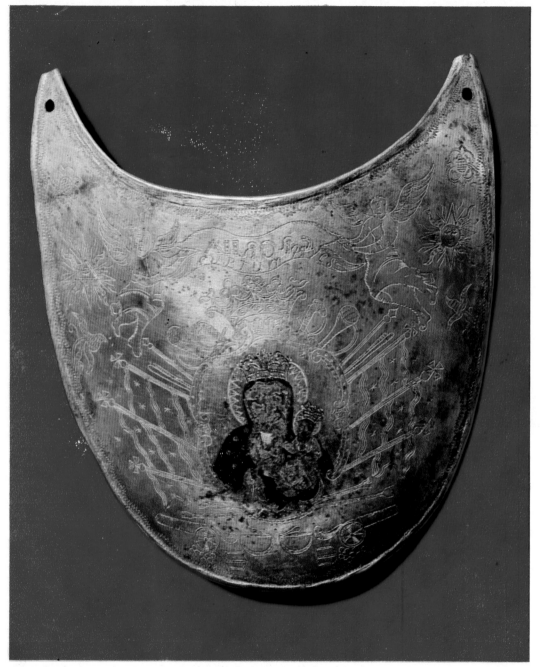

Bar Confederates' breast-plate, circa 1768-1772
Bar Confederates' Cross awarded to Casimir Pułaski at Jasna Góra on February 2nd, 1771. Our Lady of Częstochowa on the obverse side. The Arsenal
Bar Confederates' Cross with the Polish Eagle on the reverse side

Miniature neo-Gothic chapel, altar
and casket made by Tadeusz Kościuszko during his imprisonment by
the Tsar after the Insurrection.
Treasury

The battle for the monastery of Jasna Góra was an episode in the war with Sweden in which the local population, side by side with the clergy, showed steadfast courage. Father Kordecki, Prior of the heroic Monastery and commander of its garrison, described his experience in a work to which he gave the Latin title of *New Gigantomachia*. This title is an allusion to a work by the Roman poet Claudianus based on the ancient Greek myth extolling the heroic struggle of the gods of Olympus, led by Zeus and Athene, against the giants. The work was given a few editions in the 17th and first half of the 18th century. The original manuscript is preserved in the Jasna Góra library.

Not so long ago there arouse a minor sensation in learned circles in connection with *Gigantomachia*; a literary analysis of the text carried out by E. Jelonek revealed a marked duality in the style of the work. The simple narrative of Father Kordecki is interwoven with totally different baroque alterations introduced, it may be assumed, by the eventual editor, Father Stefan Damalewicz, secretary to Queen Maria Louise, Doctor of Theology.

The most important events of the siege were also faithfully transmitted to us in paint. Shortly after the departure of Swedish troops a great panoramic picture of the recent events was painted. It hangs above the grille which separates the presbytery from the main body of the Chapel of Our Lady. Another painting of the siege hangs in the Knights' Hall. It adds many details to our knowledge of the events and many valuable items of information on contemporary weapons and military strategy.

Many engravings of the siege were made and distributed all over the country. Jan Aleksander Gorczyn, a well-known graphic artist, made a copperplate panoramic engraving of the siege, which is a valuable contribution to our knowledge of Polish military history. This and the other engravings are of great value to students of historical geography and the history of Polish architecture. Alongside a panorama of Jasna Góra they display the urban settlement of Częstochowa and adjoining villages. Alongside the Swedish army besieging Jasna Góra, an outline of the Gothic church which was later converted into a baroque basilica is shown in the background.

The Bar Confederacy was another important historical event in which Jasna Góra was involved. It was here that Casimir Puławski, Polish and United States national hero, repulsed repeated attacks by Tsarist troops from September 1770 on. As the expeditionary corps dispatched by Catherine the Great was approaching Częstochowa in the late Autumn of 1770, Puławski shut himself up with troops at Jasna Góra and prepared the garrison for a last, victorious defence.

The defence of Jasna Góra during the Bar Confederacy was a final upsurge of independent Poland. After forcing the Russian troops to withdraw, Puławski left Częstochowa and shortly after emigrated abroad, never to return to the country again.

A memento of the national hero, connected with the siege, is preserved at Jasna Góra. This is the Cross of Bar Confederates, a military decoration most probably awarded to Puławski for his defence of Częstochowa, on February 2nd, 1771, the Feast of Our Lady of the Candles. The Cross preserved in the Jasna Góra treasury is one of the few examples in existence. It is not certain whether the decoration was awarded to Puławski by the High Command of the Confederation, its highest authority, or whether Puławski, aiming to take over dictatorship, himself created a prototype of the Confederates' Cross and presented it as a votive offering at the foot of the miraculous picture. It is known that after the example of other dictators, Puławski did in fact establish a military decoration, to be awarded for special merit, but its aspect remains unknown and there is no certainty it was ever awarded. Be that as it may the Cross of Casimir Puławski, steeped in mystery, is preserved in the Jasna Góra treasury. The inscription on it leaves no doubt that it belonged to Puławski. Other keepsakes, which belonged to the great national hero, Tadeusz Kościuszko, come from only a few years later. They were made by Kościuszko himself, while in Tsarist captivity, after the suppression of the 1794 Uprising.

Painting and Artistic Manufacture

HE interior furnishings at Jasna Góra can be divided into two main groups at least. The first group would consist of ornamental and utility objects destined for interiors appertaining to the cult and for the Monastery living premises, the second group would comprise various works of art, often quite unique, keepsakes and national heirlooms, presented to the Monastery as votive offerings in the course of centuries. Hence, on the one hand we have paintings, church ornaments and accessories, furniture in the various interiors and paintings, and on the other hand the votive offerings which have been constantly flowing in since the Monastery was founded. Those latter objects can be divided into smaller groups, according to their nature and destination.

As concerns furniture and accessories, not many of the original have been preserved to this day. In course of time they succumbed to the constant wear and tear and had to be replaced. On the other hand many pictures have been preserved, some of which were ordered expressly for the Monastery and add considerably to our knowledge of the history of 17th and 18th century painting in Poland.

Several main groups of paintings can be distinguished. In the first group scenes showing the history of the Order and the ideals of monastic life are pictured. The second group depicts important events in the history of Jasna Góra. The third is concerned with purely religious subjects, namely Catholic theology and the fundamental dogmas of the Faith, naturally including the ones connected with the Virgin Mary.

As concerns paintings on religious and historical subjects, the most interesting are the ones which came from the workshop of Tomaso Dolabella and his school. That great painter from Venice came to Poland at the time of Sigismund III and settled here permanently, about the year 1600. In the course of a quarter-century, he created a great school of painting. His earliest works, so far unknown to historians of art, are at Jasna Góra, where he painted frescoes in the presbytery of the Chapel of Our Lady round about 1609. The

King Casimir the Jagiellonian and his sons received into the Jasna Góra Confraternity. School of Tomaso Dolabella, painted in the first half of the 17th century. The Arsenal

F. IACOBVS PROVINCALIS P.LO
NIAE CASIMIRṼ REGEM POLẼNIA
WLADISLAṼ BOEMIAE S CASI
MIRVM CONFESSOREM AL
BERTṼ ALEXANDRṼ SIGIS
MVDṼ FRIDERICVM TVNC
PRINCIPES POLONIAE AD
MERITA ORDINIS PROTO
EREMITICI ADMITTIT
A D 1477

St. Stanislaus resurrecting Piotrowin, painted by Brother Tyburcy Nowakowic. Jasna Góra School, circa 1622. The Arsenal

Pope John XXII granting the Rule of St. Augustine to the Paulite Order in 1319; Jasna Góra School, 1st half of the 17th century. The Arsenal

B. F. LAVRENTIVS A
IOANNE XXII. REGV
LAM D. AVGVSTINI
PROMOVENTE CAROLO
REGE VNGARIÆ, PRO
ORDINE PAVLINO IMPE
TRAT ET PRIMVS OR
DINIS GENERALIS CRE
ATVR A: 1319.

B.F. THOMAS DIACON,
DVM EPISTOLAM CA
NIT AD ALTARE, IN
EXTASIM RAPITVR
ET DIVINITVS MOR
TEM SVAM ADESSE
INTELLIGENS, EAN
DEM IN SVMMA PIE
TATE LÆTVS
EXCIPIT.

picture of the Mother of God Fighting off Heresy, which hangs on the wall over the grill in that chapel is of a somewhat later date and carries the unmistakable stamp of his brush. The painting, known as " The Communion of the Jagiellonians," shows King Casimir of the Jagiellonian Dynasty and his sons, being received into the Jasna Góra Confraternity. It is one of the most interesting historical paintings in Jasna Góra and it bears distinctive marks of Dolabella's style. For an art historian studying the history of Jasna Góra art, the picture is particularly interesting from an iconographic point of view, since it shows details of the Late Renaissance ornamentation of the altar in the Chapel of Our Lady and the picture of Our Lady, unobscured by jewelled robes. Besides, the picture is painted under the influence of contemporary political trends, which traced the dynastic policy of the Vasas to Jagiellonian traditions. In it, the Jagiellonians are portrayed with the characteristic features of Vasa kings: Sigismund III, Władysław IV and John Casimir.

Another extremely interesting painting, which undoubtedly originated from Dolabella's workshop, shows King Louis of Hungary receiving the relics of St. Paul the Hermit, patriarch of the Paulite Order, brought over from Venice to Buda in 1381. The picture, important from the point of view of the Order's history, presents events in sequence. It is the centre-piece of an exhibition of Sarmatian art organised by the Paulite Monks in the Jasna Góra Arsenal.

The work of Brother Tyburcy Nowakowic, one of the few Paulite artists at Jasna Góra whose name has come down to us, also carries the stamp of Tomaso Dolabella's school. Several of his paintings have been preserved at Jasna Góra. There may have been others but the unfortunate 19th century custom of repainting pictures, prevents any accurate knowledge of his style and colour today. His most notable works are: St. Augustin, a painting of five saints with St. Isidore the Ploughman in the forefront, signed and dated 1621, and finally the painting of St. Stanislaus resurrecting the Knight of Piotrawno, showing the Church on Skałka in the background. This picture is extremely interesting to students of Cracow's history, since it shows the part-Romanesque part-Gothic outline of the church, before its conversion to the Baroque.

Death in ecstasy of the Blessed Deacon Thomas; Jasna Góra School lst half of the 17th century. The Arsenal

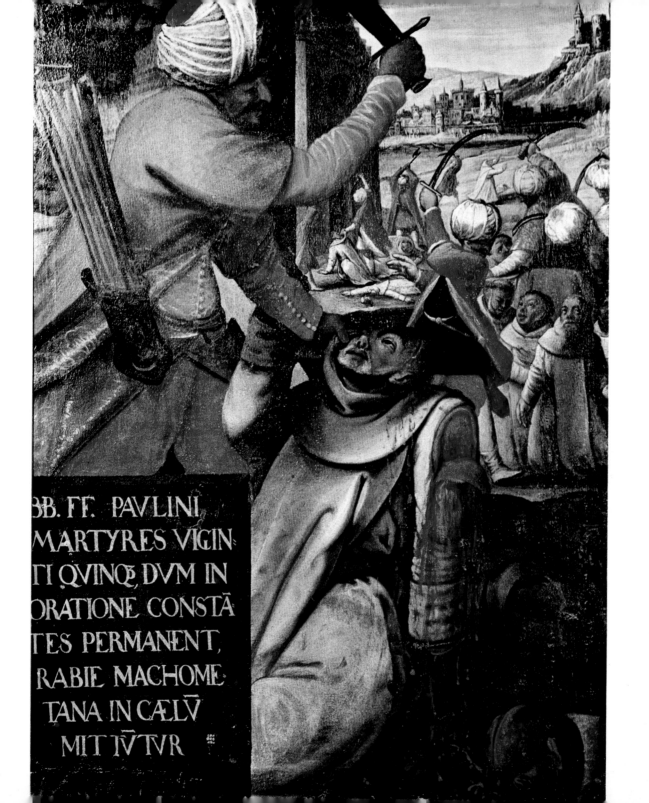

BB. FF. PAVLINI
MARTYRES VIGIN
TI QVINQ, DVM IN
ORATIONE CONSTÃ
TES PERMANENT,
RABIE MACHOME
TANA IN CÆLV̄
MIT IV̄TVR

Among the many 17th century paintings which have been preserved at Jasna Góra, the series of paintings from the second quarter of that century, showing the history of the Paulite order, is the most interesting. They are the work of several anonymous artists, whose long period of activity, at present known as the Jasna Góra school of painting, is the subject of detailed study. The series represents Paulite saints, beatified and saintly members of the Order. It is a specific kind of a gallery of antecedents, characteristic of Sarmatian taste, destined for the Monastery passages. At present, some of them are on exhibit in the Arsenal.

They display the saintly antecedents of the Paulites at Jasna Góra, beginning with Hungarian hermits headed by Andrzej (Andrew) Żurawko who lived in the 11th century, and later superiors of the Order, up to the half of the 16th century. Forty-two excellent paintings in magnificent colours, showing great depth of landscape, have been preserved to this day. In Polish conditions this is an exceptional gallery, all the more valuable since despite advanced studies on Polish painting of the first half of the 17th century only a few works have been preserved, which throw some light on that period. A series of pictures in the Knights' Hall, all undoubtedly of the school of Tomaso Dolabella, is another group of particularly noteworthy 17th century paintings, awaiting a special monographic treatise. Their importance is enhanced by the fact that they throw some light on the work of Polish continuators of the school of the Venetian master, previously unknown, who were active during the second half of the 17th century. The series comprises nine paintings representing more important events in the history of Jasna Góra and connected with historical processes and events of more general significance. We see in turn the act of foundation of the Monastery at Jasna Góra, Duke Władysław of Opole presenting the picture of Our Lady, the sacrilegious Hussite attempt, King Władysław IV Vasa rendering homage and thanksgiving at Jasna Góra for the victory of Chocim, the siege of Jasna Góra by the Swedish army, John Casimir receiving at the Knights' Hall the homage of the Zaporozche cossacks against the background of the panorama of Toruń liberated from the Swedes, the wedding ot King Michael Korybut celebrated at

Murder of Paulite Monks in Hungary during the Turkish invasion of 1526; Jasna Góra School, lst half of the 17th century. The Arsenal

VLADISLAVS IV. POLONIARVM PRIN
CEPS. HIC AD ARAM THAVMATVRGÆ VIR
GINIS. BELLI SVMPTIS AVSPICIIS SVB CHO
CIMENSI ARCE CVM SERENISSIMO SIGIS
MVNDO PARENTE. OSMANVM TVRCARVM
TYRANNVM PAVCIS SVIS DESIDERATIS
GLORIOSISSIME DECIES REPETITA
ACIE. PROFLIGAT REDENS IN GRATI
TVDINIS TESSERAM MONASTERIVM
HOC QVATVOR PROPVGNACVLI

Future King Władysław IV Vasa,
offering up thanksgiving at Jasna
Góra for the victory at Chocim in
1621; painting from the cycle on
the history of Jasna Góra; 2nd half
of the 17th century. Knights' Hall

King John Casimir receiving the homage of Toruń burghers after the liberation of the town from the Swedes; painting from the cycle on the history of Jasna Góra. End of the 17th century. Knights' Hall

Wedding ceremony of King Michael Korybut Wiśniowiecki and Eleonora, Archduchess of Austria celebrated at Jasna Góra in 1670; from the cycle on the history of Jasna Góra. End of the 17th century. Knights' Hall

King John III Sobieski setting off to the relief of Vienna in 1683; fragment of the picture showing Paulite Monks offering the sword of Hetman Żółkiewski to the King; from the cycle on the history of Jasna Góra. End of the 17th century. Knights' Hall

Jasna Góra, the relief of Vienna by John III Sobieski, coming of the relics of Saints Honorata and Candyda and the fire which damaged the Monastery Church in 1690. The Częstochowa fire-brigade galloping to the rescue of the burning church shown in the background has great power of expression and force of movement. The third series of 17th century paintings, hanging in the Sacristy, also represents a high artistic standard. It shows scenes from the history of eremites and early hermits, not only of the Paulite Order. What makes it even more interesting is that it shows among others, hermits from Asia Minor, whose cult was rarely observed in Poland. The paintings of considerable size show the story of St. Sophronia the Hermit, St. Dythna Princess of Scotland, medieval founder of mental homes who was one of the first to take care of the mentally sick, St. Romuald in his hermitage, St. Mary the Egyptian, Primitius on the island and the most outstanding work of the lot, showing the temptation of St. Anthony. The Saint, surrounded by temptations personified, is attacked with a crampon by Satan. The scene is presented against a background of the ruins of an ancient temple, in a disturbing, strangely contrasting, sinister light. The figure of Vanity, in the guise of a naked woman with butterfly wings holding a mirror in her hand, is shown against the temple ruins. The subject matter of the above cycle indicates a close affinity with 17th century Spanish mysticism, which exercised a strong influence on the spiritual life of the Polish Paulites.

The Sacristy, completed in 1651. General view of the interior. Ceiling frescoes by Karl Dankwart completed after 1693. The Sacristy cupboards and pictures are from the 2nd half of the 17th century. The Sacrilegious Communion is seen on the west wall, the Martyrdom of St. Dythna, Thaïs Penitent and the Communion of Mary the Egyptian are on the north wall

Primitius on the Island, about the mid-17th century; the Sacristy, south wall

Temptation of St. Anthony,
mid-17th century; the Sacristy, south wall

PROCENIE CLARVS VIRTVTE ANTONIVS ART
PAVPERIBVS LARGVS SORRIETATIS AMANS
CASTA PVS MISCET PRECIBVS IEIVNIA ET AB

VIRGA PARENS FLORIS QVEM SPÍRÍTVS ÎLE CORONAT,
NOS TÎBÍ TE NOBÍS ÎNSERVÎSSE VELÍS .

The Tree of Jesse; about the mid-17th century. Refectory Vestibule, painted panel

Our Lady of Succour protecting a town besieged by dismounted ranks of the enemy; mid-17th century. Refectory Vestibule, painted door panel from cupboard formerly in Treasury

DIVA, NEC IGNITIS PENETRABILIS VMBO SAGIT[T]
HOSTICA IN AVCTORIS TELA RETVNDE CAPVT

The Virgin Mary — Protectress of Sinners; mid-17th century. The Arsenal. Picture on painted panel

Pictures which were part of former church fixtures represent lesser artistic value, but are rich in essence and interesting from the point of view of Marian iconography. There are about twenty of them. Painted in oil paints on wood, they display Marian themes of extremely complex iconography based on a Jesuit theological treatise. Very probably they used to form the back of monks' cells. All of them are from the first half of the 17th century. Two of the pictures are of special interest to students of history, particularly to students of military history. One shows the Mother of God in the guise of a Fortified Camp, the other as a City beleaguered by dismounted ranks of the enemy. Almost the whole arsenal of contemporary weapons can be distinguished in them. The statuette of the Virgin Mary symbolised as the Protectress of Sinners is a typically Sarmatian representation.

As concerns wall painting on the vaulted ceilings and walls of Jasna Góra Monastery, the great series of paintings executed in 1690—1693 by Karl Dankwart, on the Basilica ceiling, deserves first mention. The series is composed of two groups: the history of the finding of the Holy Cross is painted in the presbytery and the history of the picture of Our Lady and the miracles she performed at Jasna Góra, in the main body of the Basilica. It represents events noted in the Monastery chronicles. One fresco shows the miraculous escape of miners buried in the silver mines at Olkusz, an event which echoed throughout medieval Poland. Another shows a hanged child being restored to life. Karl Dankwart, the artist, displayed his own likeness on one of the frescoes. According to Monastery chronicles, he was a Swede who settled in Nysa, Silesia and was converted to Catholicism.

The collection of objects of the goldsmith's art and ornamental fabrics is extremely rich. Some of the earliest and most valuable objects date back to the 15th century. The collection of ancient objects of the goldsmith's art must have been vast indeed, as proved by church inventories, which have been preserved from the 17th century on. Unfortunately only few of the Gothic period furnishings remain. Subjected to constant wear and tear due to the flocking crowds of pilgrims, they did not last as long as elsewhere and were replaced by new furnishings in the style of the given period.

Nowadays one can only surmise at the class of workmanship represented by Gothic objects of the goldsmith's art and ornamental fabrics, from the few which have been preserved to this day. The so-called Hungarian Chasuble is one of them. As tradition has it, it was brought to Częstochowa from Hungary by the Paulite Monks. The workmanship is not earlier than the second half of the 15th century. It is a magnificent example of the so-called architectonic style of embroidery, in which certain parts stand out from the background to form a three-dimensional artistic composition. Scenes of the Annunciation, and the Dormition of the Virgin Mary are represented on the chasuble, as well as St. Paul the Apostle and St. Paul the Hermit protecting the person of the donor and her children, a member of the Hungarian Drughet family, as proved by the crest embroidered below. This family was related to the Batorys, which may also have been the reason why the chasuble found its way to Jasna Góra. It is worth noting that the architectonic canopies crowning each of the scenes, protrude several centimetres above the fabric. Robes in which the figures are adorned are thickly studded with pearls. The precious material on which the embroidery is executed, was manufactured in Italy, probably in Venice.

Two other chasubles from the Gothic period have been preserved. The first dates from the turn of the 15th century and is considered a work of art of high artistic value. Similarly to the one described above, it has a cross column of figures, representing scenes after the Dutch master Roger van der Weyden and his circle. It depicts the Crucifixion with Our Lady standing at the foot of the Cross, supported by St. John and St. Mary Magdalene. This work of Cracow embroidery is a gift from a vicar of St. Mary's Church in Cracow.

Another chasuble from the second decade of the 16th century has scenes of the Annunciation and Nativity embroidered in relief, after the etchings of Albrecht Dürer. This permits us to establish the exact date of its execution.

Very few objects of medieval goldsmithery have been preserved, moreover they come from the early 16th century. The great, Late Gothic monstrance, donated by Sigismund the Old, made in 1542, as proved by the date stamped on the base, is probably of Cracow workmanship. Tradition holds that Sigis-

The Annunciation, detail from late 15th century chasuble of Hungarian workmanship. The cross-column embroidered in gold and silver thread and pearls

15th century chasuble presented by the Archpresbyter of St. Mary's Church in Cracow. Embroidered with the scene of the Crucifixion. The Treasury

Our Lady of the Apocalypse,
detail from chasuble dating from
1510. The Treasury

Monstrance offered by King Sigismund I in 1542. Probably of Polish workmanship. The Treasury

Figure of the Sorrowing Christ, the Monstrance offered by King Sigismund I, detail

mund the Old himself made it, but in fact it is the work of a professional, albeit anonymous, goldsmith.

The great altar cross with the figures of the Sorrowful Mother of Christ and St. John, is also a gift bestowed by King Sigismund I. The Crucifix is the signed work of a Nuremberg artist, dated 1510, and represents art of the highest quality. A sceptre embossed with rock crystal, executed about the year 1500, is another royal gift.

Traditions of Gothic art may also be observed in two reliquary crosses, which however are probably of 17th century workmanship. Several other valuable objects date from the 16th century. First among them are precious material from which liturgical vestments were made. Detailed lists of "apparatus" or complete sets of liturgical vestments and of the precious stones they contain, are preserved in the Monastery archives, thanks to which the names of many of the donors are known.

An "apparatus" of great value was offered by Queen Bona Sforza, spouse of Sigismund I. The material is of Italian workmanship of the highest quality, dating from the end of the Gothic and beginning of the Renaissance period. This Genoese cloth-of-gold arouses the admiration of experts and connoisseurs to this day. The material has its own "pedigree." The cloth-of-gold was a wedding gift to Bona, offered by her royal consort Sigismund the Old, hence it must date back to the beginning of the 16th century. It is woven in diamond pattern with flower rosettes in the middle. Threads taken from pieces at either end of the fabric are knotted to form the rosettes. The pattern symbolises the tie of marriage and the knots symbolise the royal couple's married bliss and the union between two reigning houses. It is that cloth-of-gold from which the "apparatus" with a cope and chasuble preserved until today were made. Its value is enhanced by fragments of goldware sewn on to it, which include parts of diadems or crowns which had probably belonged to the Jagiellonians.

Other valuable objects of the goldsmith's art include a Late Gothic cross wrought in crystal, presented by Cardinal Andrzej Batory.

King Sigismund I presenting the reliquary crucifix and monstrance to the Pauline Monks. School of Jasna Góra, 2nd half of the 17th century. The Arsenal

Reliquary Crucifix offered by King Sigismund I. Nuremberg workmanship from 1510. The Treasury

Figure of Our Lady, detail from the reliquary crucifix

Figure of St. John the Evangelist, detail from the reliquary crucifix

The figure of Our Lady of the Immaculate Conception, presented in 1604 by the Abbot of the Cistercian Monks in Oliwa, is an outstanding example of amber workmanship.

But most of the objects in the Monastery treasury date from after the Swedish "deluge," when the fame of Jasna Góra as an impregnable fortress was at its highest. A magnificent gold monstrance, known as "Kordecki's Monstrance" ornamented in coloured enamel and set with a great number of precious stones is a collective offering presented in commemoration of that historical event. The work of a Warsaw goldsmith, Wacław Grotke, it was executed in 1672. Its great size, multi-coloured ornaments and the sumptuous splendour of the materials used, fully reflect the Sarmatian taste of the period.

There are also many gifts testifying to royal munificence. The so-called "coral set," a complete set of vessels used during celebration of the mass, the work of an anonymous Venetian goldsmith, entrances the eye by the elegant beauty of its workmanship. It was presented by King Michael Korybut Wiśniowiecki on the occasion of his wedding at Jasna Góra and consists of a chalice, two ampullae, salvers and two ciboriums, one for preserving the Holy Eucharist, the other for Holy Oils.

Other offerings presented by Michael Korybut are to be found at Jasna Góra. They include works by Augsburg goldsmiths among which the most arresting is the monstrance offered by the Empress Eleonora, mother of the royal spouse. The monstrance is of a very original design. It consists of a column wrought from a single block of rock crystal set in a magnificent pedestal studded with precious stones. It also had a small figure of Christ at the Column, but unfortunately this was lost. Two gilt and enamelled candlesticks set with precious and semi-precious stones must also be mentioned. Works of gold-smithery of this class are only to be seen in the greatest European collections, and in Poland the collection is quite unique. Numerous old inventories in existence prove that in former times precious objects could be found even in burghers' homes to say nothing of the manor houses of the gentry or the palaces of the aristocracy, but the numerous wars with their looting and devastation, deprived the country of most of its treasures of this class.

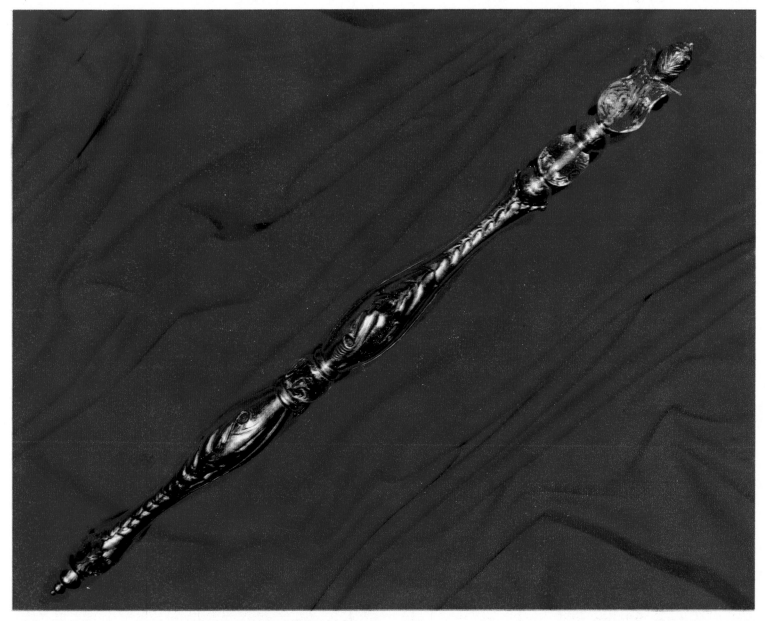

Sceptre of the Jagiellonians offered by King Sigismund I,
made in 1500. The Treasury

Detail of chasuble from the "Apparatus" offered by Queen Bona. Sides in cloth-of-gold, fragments of Jagiellonian crowns sown on the centre column. Early 16th century. The Treasury

Amber statuette of the Immaculate Virgin Mary. 16th/17th century, offered by the Cistercian Abbot of Oliwa in 1604. The Treasury

The Kordecki Monstrance, the work of the Warsaw goldsmith Wacław Grotke, executed in 1672

Chalice, ampullae and plate belonging to the Coral Set, 17th century Venetian workmanship. Wedding offering of King Michael Korybut Wiśniowiecki presented in 1670. The Treasury

The precious jewel-box offered by Queen Marysieńka Sobieska and converted in 1727 to hold the relic of St. John Nepomucen is of Augsburg workmanship. Truly royal gifts from the first half of the 18th century were offered by members of the Wettin Dynasty reigning in Poland at the time. They include two crystal vases, of Augsburg workmanship, set on jewel-studded pedestals, and a Renaissance crystal reliquary cross with Baroque ornamentations, presented by Queen Josephine, spouse of August III. An extremely valuable set of white Meissen porcelain consisting of figures of the Apostles, two crucifixes, chandeliers and a chalice was a gift of the King.

Among other 18th century objects in the collection a jewelled and enamelled chalice offered by Franciszek Ferdynand Lubomirski in 1752, deserves special mention. Of Augsburg workmanship, it was executed in 1743. The crosier or pastoral staff, from the first half of the 18th century of Prior Konstanty Moszyński, famous patron of the arts and benefactor of the Monastery, also catches the eye. Jasna Góra is indebted to Father Moszyński for two of the most imposing sets of liturgical vestments in its possession. The first is known as the "Pearl Apparatus" because of the great number of pearls which went into its making. It was made from votive offerings in 1726. Tradition holds that the many-coloured velvet material from which the intricate pattern which serves as background for the different items was made, came from the cloak of Prince Jakub Sobieski. The second apparatus was donated only a year later by Michał Krassowski, Canon of Warsaw, eminent theologian, writer and scholar. The circumstances in which the "Krassowski Apparatus" came into existence and its complex iconography will be discussed in detail in the second part of this work.

In addition to objects of utility, several hundred votive offerings of metal sheets in gold and silver form a separate part of the collection. Some of them represent great artistic value, others are touching in their naive simplicity. Among the most noteworthy is the one offered in 1650 by Jan Chreptowicz, in thanksgiving for regaining his freedom from captivity, after the defeat at Żółte Wody in 1648. A votive offering presented by the City of Vilna in 1711 is valuable for students of the iconography of the city.

Wedding offerings presented by the Habsburgs on the occasion of the wedding of Eleonora, Archduchess of Austria to King Michael Korybut Wiśniowiecki in 1670. Crystal Monstrance offered by the Empress Eleonora and a pair of chandeliers by Maria Anna, the Archduchess Eleonora's sister. 17th century Augsburg workmanship. The Treasury

Offerings flowing into the Monastery over the centuries were systematically preserved in the Jasna Góra treasury. After a time, the most valuable ones were set apart and taken out of use, thanks to which they have lasted to this day.

Prior to 1900 the treasury at Jasna Góra was arranged to form a museum — which at the time was proof of quite modern ideas. An exhibition was organised and made accessible to visitors. A guide was also provided. This fine tradition has been upheld by the Paulite monks. In recent years a new museum wing has been opened, housing a section of the Treasury known as the Treasury-Arsenal. The Arsenal building, used as a storehouse ever since it stopped serving its original purpose, was fitted out to house a very interesting exhibition organised along most modern lines, according to the project of Professor Bohdan Urbanowicz and his assistants, Jan Lis and Witold Chróś-cicki. The most valuable objects for which no room could be found in the old Treasury are exhibited there. Valuable ornamental fabrics, 17th century paintings of the so-called Jasna Góra School, military exhibits and a collection of musical instruments. There are also some rare examples of orders and decorations, such as the Order of the Golden Fleece on a richly ornamented chain offered by Władysław IV, the previously mentioned Bar Confederates' Cross, votive offering of Casimir Pułaski, and the anonymous gift of a Virtuti Militari Cross from 1792. A group of coffin portraits and epitaphs painted on metal, are on display in the Arsenal. Shown in the Exhibition of Polish Art in London in 1970, the portraits created a sensation among art connoisseurs. This type of painting was known only in Poland. It formed part of Sarmatian funeral rites in the Baroque period. The coffin portraits and epitaphs preserved at Jasna Góra are connected with some of the greatest Polish families. They will be discussed in greater detail in the second part of this work.

In addition to works of art of great value, authentic national heirlooms connected with Poland's history were saved for posterity at Jasna Góra, regardless of their artistic or intrinsic value. Military heirlooms belong to this category. Their collection is rendered all the more valuable by the fact that it

Detail from one of the two crystal vases offered in 1744 by Maria Josephine, spouse of August III, King of Poland and Saxony. 17th/18th century Augsburg workmanship. The Treasury

Crystal Reliquary Crucifix. Renaissance with 17th/18th century ornamentations. Gift of Queen Maria Josephine, spouse of August III, King of Poland and Saxony. The Treasury

St. Andrew Apostle. Meissen china figure by Joachim Kändler executed between 1737 and 1740. Gift of August III King of Poland and Saxony, offered in 1747. The Treasury

Jewel studded chalice with six enamelled plates showing scenes of
Our Lord's Passion. Offered by Franciszek Ferdynand Lubomirski in
1752. The Treasury

Crosier used by Prior Konstanty Moszyński, Livonain bishop, 1st quarter of the 18th century. The Treasury

Cope and chasuble belonging to the Pearl Apparatus, offered by Prior Konstanty Moszyński in 1728. Multi-coloured appliqué satinwork from the cloak of Prince Jakub Sobieski, with a design in precious stones and pearls from votive offerings. The Arsenal

112

Votive offering of Jan Chreptowicz, fragment

was amassed from spontaneous offerings. Many items are connected with outstanding historical figures or with the most important events in Polish history. The collection includes many military trophies of great value. Among the magnificent examples of weapons, to which a separate chapter of this work is devoted, a group of 17th century oriental guns, which according to tradition were part of the booty taken by John III Sobieski at Vienna, arouses special interest.

Other oriental military equipment, rarely to be seen in European collections, also captured at Vienna, comprises ornamental shields, bows and quivers of different type, as well as a rare "Bunchuk," symbol of military authority, equivalent to a banner. Used in Turkish and Tartar armies, it took the form of a horse's tail set on the cross-section of a staff. Parts of Turkish tents made of materials woven in ornate designs, are most striking among the booty

Votive silver plate offered by Jan Chreptowicz, son of the Palatine of Novgorod, in 1650 in thanksgiving for his release from Tartar captivity after the defeat of Żółte Wody in 1648. The Treasury

114

captured at Vienna. Such materials were highly valued in 17th century Poland. Sobieski offered many as a decoration for the Chapel of Our Lady at Jasna Góra. Only a few of them remain today. The most valuable are two magnificent tent-sides, embroidered in gold and silver thread. According to local tradition they formed part of the tent used by the Grand Vizier, Kara Mustafa himself. The Sarmatian taste for oriental fabrics was reflected in the Polish nobleman's dress. Broad belts woven in intricate, eastern patterns, were an essential element of the national costume. Their manufacture on a large scale began in Poland in the 18th century. Several such belts to be admired in the Jasna Góra collection were made by such well-known artists of the craft as Franciszek Selimand, Paschalis Jakubowicz and Jakub Puciłowski.

Old musical instruments in the Arsenal Exhibition, once used by the Jasna Góra orchestra, attract great interest. A separate chapter is devoted to the history of this orchestra, which testified to the high standard of music performed in the Monastery.

In accordance with ancient tradition, every monastery of greater importance was also the intellectual centre of the whole region and possessed a library. The library was usually located in representative apartments, which provided a proper setting. At Jasna Góra literary traditions were cherished almost from the beginning. Its medieval library was gradually increased over successive centuries. The disastrous fire in 1690 destroyed the greater part of the collection, causing irreparable loss to Polish culture.

The original site of the library is uncertain, but it is known that like all other contemporary libraries it consisted of three main sections. The first contained liturgical books used during religious services, such as Missals, Antiphonaries, Rituals etc. The second contained schoolbooks. It must be remembered that every more important monastery had its own school. The third section contained documents, law books, legal codes and the archives, accumulated in the course of centuries. It should be noted that many of the older books were printed by the Monastery printing press, which remained in operation for two centuries. Books were also brought over from other Paulite branches in Poland and abroad mainly from Venice and Nuremberg.

Votive silver plate presented by the city of Lvov in 1717. The Treasury

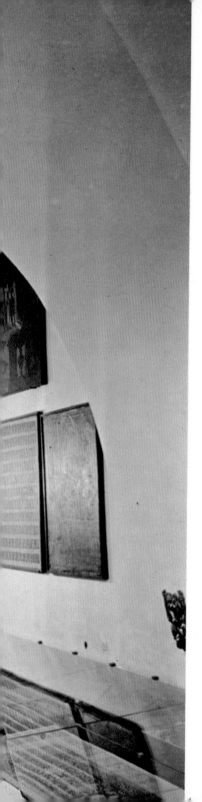

When Father Moszyński set about rebuilding the Monastery and church, after the fire, premises were set aside for the library, on the first floor of the new southern wing. Carpentry work was completed in 1739. Brother Grzegorz Woźniakowic, the Monastery's wood-carver, made the library into a harmonious, compact whole. The bookshelves blended with the panelling to form a distinguished, harmonious interior. Two great library tables with ornamental marquetry work in different coloured woods arouse admiration to this day. Each has a medallion in the centre. One shows the meeting between St. Paul and St. Anthony, the other the figure of St. Thomas Aquinas.

The allegorical painting on the Library ceiling represents Theology as the Queen of all Sciences. The side medallions extol the contemplative and scholarly life, others represent godly and ungodly pastimes. Gambling was included among the ungodly ones.

The Library contains a large part of the original collection at Jasna Góra, which was saved from the fire. Medieval school-type manuscripts number over two hundred. Though unpretentious, written on ordinary paper and bound in simple, heavy covers, they contain much interesting information. For instance Monastery historians found that one of the manuscripts contains a copy of the earliest text of the history of the miraculous picture (known as "The Transportation of the Picture"). This copy of the original manuscript from the turn of the 14th century was executed in 1470. There is also a rare copy of St. Augustine's monastic rule, dating from the end of the 15th century. The collection of diplomas, grants and privileges bestowed on the Monastery is quite unique and there are more than fifty of them, with all their seals intact.

The earliest document is the Act of Foundation, by Władysław Duke of Opole, issued on the 22nd of June, 1382 and bearing his majestic seal, which

The Arsenal. General view of the exhibition arranged according to the design of Professor Bohdan Urbanowicz, Jan Lis M.A. and Dr. Witold Chróścicki, in 1969

119

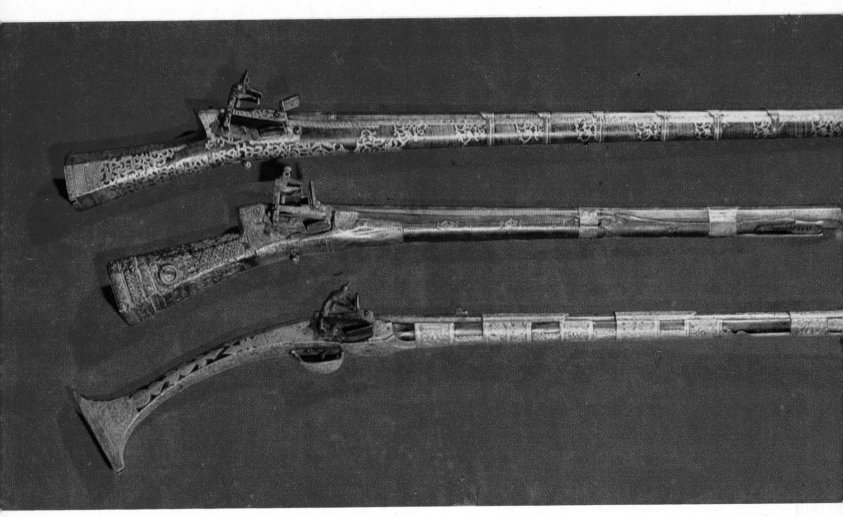

17th century Turkish rifles. The Arsenal

Small insignia of the Order of the Golden Fleece offered by King Władysław IV Vasa (1632—1648) on a richly ornamented chain of Polish workmanship. The Arsenal

Panelling over the library portal, executed by Brother Grzegorz Woźniakowic, signed and dated 1739. The Library

"Bunchuk" (horse-tailed insignia of office of Turkish military commanders) and part of Turkish tent which according to tradition was used by the Grand Vizier Kara Mustafa, offered by King John III Sobieski after his victory at Vienna in 1683. The Arsenal

is a great rarity. The seal is a Gothic work of art in miniature. In great detail it shows the figure of the Duke on horseback, clad in full armour, with a little monkey holding on to the saddle. The next is the privilege granted by Władysław Jagiełło in 1393, bearing the King's majestic seal, also of great artistic value. The collection contains a series of the seals of Cardinal Zbigniew Oleśnicki, an extremely rare seal of King John Albert, one of King Alexander the Jagiellon and a fine, varied collection of Mazovian seals.

The seal of the Warsaw Confraternity of St. Anne from the 17th century is a great curiosity.

The Library. Fragment of the fresco showing the Paulite monks in a dispute

The Library, view of the south wall and ceiling frescoes. Allegoric representation of the peace and harmony of Music, symbolic composition "Wisdom — the Greatest Power" and two Paulite monks in a theological dispute

Three volumes of the "Book of Miracles" are preserved at Jasna Góra. They contain reports on miracles performed through the intercession of the picture of Our Lady listed from the beginning of the 16th century up to the end of the 18th century. In the mid-18th century the volumes were decorated with naive, amateur drawings, which nonetheless are full of expression and not devoid of a specific charm. They were executed by Father Innocent Pokorski, the Monastery archivist, an educated and widely-travelled man. The drawings show every Paulite monastery in Poland, hence they are important to the history of Paulite architecture in this country. Even more

important and interesting still, some of the drawings represent historical events. One shows the election of King Stanisław Leszczyński, another shows the "castrum doloris" set up in the Chapel of Our Lady during the obsequies after the death of Voivode Stanisław Warszycki. Yet another shows Warsaw besieged by the Swedes, in the next the Swedish commander, General Horn, is seen surrendering to King Stanisław Leszczyński in the Court of Honour of the Royal Castle in Warsaw. All the drawings were executed in pen and ink, in amateur fashion, and lightly touched up with water-colours. The Jasna Góra Library also contains works of professional artists, some of which may be considered real masterpieces. They add greatly to our knowledge of art and culture in the Jagiellonian period. Objects saved from fire in 1690 include extremely rare illuminated manuscripts. The earliest is a Bible dating from the first quarter of the 15th century. A miniature painting begins each new chapter of the Bible. The most striking one is the figure of Ruth wearing a low-cut court dress, her golden hair loosened over her shoulders, gathering ears of corn in the field of her kinsman Booz, into a wicker basket. The margins of the Bible pages are peopled with the symbolic world of Gothic fauna : a running hare, a stork about to take wing, a devil with a woman's head, seen approaching David's sickbed... A later work, an Italian breviary, probably of Venetian workmanship, would bring honour to any of the greatest collections of illuminated manuscripts in the world. It was probably brought to Jasna Góra from a Paulite Monastery in Hungary. However, that may be, it must be counted among the supreme achievements of the illuminating art in Europe. The delicate, translucid parchment was made from skins of unborn lambs. Its parchment pages are illuminated in delicate fairy-like colours and gold. The margins are covered in tiny gold dots, with flowers weaving and butterflies flitting among them and birds drinking from the calyxes of flowers. The luxurious tangle of this enchanted garden is peopled with tiny figures of winged cherubs wearing pieces of coral round their necks, a charm which was supposed to protect infants from the evil eye during teething troubles. It is likely that the Italian illuminator concealed his signature somewhere among them. The manuscript has over seven hundred illuminated

Marquetry table from the 1st half of the 18th century, probably the work of Brother Grzegorz Woźniakowic. Figure of St. Thomas Aquinas in the centre. The Library

127

capitals, none over five centimetres square. Despite their diminutive size, the precision of the drawings, the precise application of colour, their incredible lucidity, despite the saturation of sapphire blues, purples, greens and reds, is bound to arouse admiration. Only Italian painters knew how to bring out such intensity of light.

But the best and most valuable example of Polish culture at the close of the medieval period, preserved at Jasna Góra, is a Missal which was part of the

Seal showing the equestrian figure of Władysław Duke of Opole on the Act of Foundation of the Monastery in 1382. Archives

Seal of Cardinal Zbigniew Oleśnicki on the document granting the privilege of Indulgences in 1430. Archives

splendid offering presented by King John Albert. Prostrated by mortal illness, the King presented this Missal, two others and a gradual, as a votive offering, beseeching his return to health.

As concerns liturgy, the Missal was arranged in conformance with the rule of the Paulite order. The prayers are according to the Augustinian rule. The illuminations belong to the highest level attained by that art in Poland. They are the work of at least two artists, one of whom was undoubtedly the illuminator of the Ciołek Pontifical.

The first illumination, showing King David praying, is one of the best and most valuable in the Missal. The figure of the young knight with golden curls, adorned in sumptuous armour is easily identified as King John Albert. The scene shows David praying before his contest with Goliath. This is an allusion to John Albert's heroic struggle against the whole might of Turkey. The many intricate ornamentations include a miniature of David with the date 1506 and an intricate monogram, which can be deciphered as the three letters CMC probably signifying " Clarus Mons Czestochoviensis " or Jasna Góra in Częstochowa. On the sarcophagus in the scene of the Resurrection, the artist put the date 1507 and the letters SA which can be deciphered as "Sigismundus Augustus" and concern King Sigismund the Old who carried out his brother's foundation.

The delicate design of the landscapes, the precision with which distant views of mist-shrouded mountains are rendered, the mastery with which the tiny figures are drawn, the skill with which colours are applied, the use of gold to enhance the visual effects and add splendour to the figures represented, the richness and variety of ornamental compositions, the margins filled with flowers and fruits, make the Albert Missal one of the most magnificent works of Cracow illuminators of the early 16th century.

In addition to works of historical and artistic value, the Jasna Góra Library has another important section which contains over three thousand five hundred archive volumes which escaped destruction in the disasters and looting Poland experienced during the Partition Period. When other religious houses were being closed down, when the partitioning powers were seizing the contents

Bible with the initial "I" and figure of Ruth gathering ears of wheat in her kinsman's field, Cracow work from the 1st quarter of the 15th century. Archives

Breviary with a miniature showing David with his retinue of singers outside the Temple. Italy, circa 1480. Archives

Ra
tes
mic
omes
reddi
mus
dno
deo
qui

natuutate nos liberauit de dyabo

Missal with the initial "A", offered by King John Albert. David's Prayer and a Pauline monk praying. Wawel Illumination Workshop, work of the pontifical master of Bishop Erazm Ciołek, 1506—1507. Archives

ld te leuam Et iste modus rep
cendr mttortur seruatur per to

of far more ancient libraries, like the one at Tyniec for instance, and auctioning them in various countries of Europe, Jasna Góra was taking in archival documents from various other convents and monasteries.

It is valuable material particularly as concerns the history of art, unpublished and as yet little known. Already on the basis of an introductory orientation in the stores of the Jasna Góra archives one may expect that the archives will supply important information on the history of spiritual and artistic culture in Poland.

"SILVA RERUM" AT JASNA GÓRA

A Mysterious Painting

HE exhibition of *objets d'art* in the Jasna Góra collection was opened in the Monastery Arsenal in 1969. Its dominant feature is a great painting which covers almost the whole wall facing the entrance. One of the biggest paintings in the collection, its outstanding artistic qualities and the variety of scenes represented, have long deserved special study. The event represented in the picture was known to monastery historians but it had never been studied by historians of art. The authors of this work endeavoured to solve the riddle presented by this picture and interpret its hidden significance by studying the style and method in which it is painted and investigating historical sources. The picture represents one of the most important events in the history of the Paulite Order, namely the transportation of the Relic of St. Paul the Hermit from Venice to Buda, the capital of Hungary. The solemn transportation, the Latin word used was "translatio", took place in 1381, at the instigation of Louis the Great of the House of Anjou, King of Hungary and Poland, protector and benefactor of the Paulite order. Acquisition of the relic of the First Hermit and Patriarch of the Paulite Order by Hungary, had more than a purely religious significance : the cult of the Saint who originated from Asia Minor, was connected with plans to regain the Holy Land from the Infidel, which in the eyes of contemporary Europe signified the

138

Transportation of the Relic of St. Paul the Hermit from Venice to Buda in Hungary in 1381, by Tomaso Dolabella. The picture was probably executed by order of Tomasz Zamoyski between 1628 and 1635. The Arsenal

Detail from the picture showing King Louis of Hungary and his retinue

Ottoman Turks. In addition, possession of the Relic of the Patriarch of the Order, permitted establishment of new Paulite monasteries beyond the boundaries of Hungary, thus strengthening the influence of the Realm over dependent countries. On the 22nd of June, 1382, six months after arrival of the Relic in Buda, the Paulite Monastery at Jasna Góra was founded, and a particle of the Relic was installed there. To this day, the Relic is kept in a magnificent reliquary, shaped in the from of Paulite Arms, made in the 18th century. The Paulite Arms were shaped from the legend of the life of St. Paul the Hermit. Transportation of St. Paul's Relic to Hungary and the foundation of Jasna Góra Monastery, indirectly connected with it, were events frequently depicted in various form by the Paulites in centuries to come. The painting in question comes from the second half of the 17th century, and treats of that same subject, which had become extremely pertinent, in view of the Turkish threat to Poland. Conformingly with the custom prevailing in Polish 17th century painting, concealed significance was added to the historical events represented. The figures are painted wearing contemporary costumes and accessories.

The sequence of events in the picture is shown in narrative form. Venice, its buildings and canals, is shown in detail against a broad expanse of sea, on the right of the picture. A ship under full canvas, sailing towards the city, stands out among many others swaying on the gentle swell. That is the ship Louis of Hungary dispatched to bring the Relic of St. Paul from Venice to Buda. Also on the right but close up in the foreground the ship is shown moored to the jetty, after its return. It resembles a Spanish galleon, of a type generally used at the end of the 16th and beginning of the 17th century. Figures are shown descending the gangplank towards a group of women kneeling at the quay-side. Attention is drawn by the figure of the princess, in a blue mantle and wearing a crown over her long, flowing hair. The massive outline of the royal castle in Buda is seen on the left. A procession is just leaving it, on its way to receive the Relic of the Saint. Despite the distance, the noble figure of the aged king surrounded by court dignitaries, is easily recognizable. The small kneeling figure of the princess can be none other than Jadwiga (Hedvig), daughter of Louis of Hungary, future Queen of Poland, eleven years

Reliquary in the shape of the Paulite
Coat of Arms with a relic of St. Paul
the Hermit. 18th century workmanship. The Treasury

old at the time. A close-up view of the procession is shown again this time in the foreground, carrying the Relic to the Royal chapel in the castle. Among the many anonymous figures of ecclesiastic and lay dignitaries in the procession, several historical figures are recognizable. A cardinal and an archbishop can be distinguished among the group of church dignitaries heading the procession. Their magnificent pontifical robes attest to their rank and dignity. They are Valentine des Cinque-Eglises, Cardinal and Papal Nuncio, and Paul, Archbishop of Zagreb in the pontifical robes of an Eastern Patriarch. Two ecclesiastics behind them are carrying their insignia of rank. The portrayed head of the younger, probably represents Father Andrzej Gołdonowski, Provincial of the Paulite order, who, in all likelihood, suggested the subject of the painting.

The principal figure is that of King Louis in magnificent Hungarian costume surrounded by his court, walking right behind the Relic of the Saint. Two princes are walking at the head of the royal retinue. The one on the left, wearing a gold chain and holding the Seal of State testifying to his dignity of Chancellor of the Realm, is Władysław, Duke of Opole, the King's Lieutenant and founder of the Monastery at Jasna Góra. It is characteristic that neither the King nor his Chancellor are looking towards the Relic which is the central theme of the composition. Their eyes are directed to the figure of a man, standing in the right-hand corner of the picture. The gracious gesture of the King and his Chancellor's expression, distinguish the stranger from the other witnesses of the great event. He carries no particular sign of his identity, but the head, shown in profile, is almost identical to that on portraits of Tomasz Zamoyski, son and heir of the great Chancellor Jan, defender of the Realm, who understood the danger of the Turkish threat and knew how to prevent it. Could it be that it was Tomasz Zamoyski who had the picture painted as an offering to Jasna Góra? He is known to have been one of the Monastery's chief benefactors, so this is more than likely. It is probable he had the picture painted during the period of the growing threat of invasion from Turkey between 1628 and 1635, when he was seeking appointment to the office of deputy-chancellor and later to that of Grand-Chancellor of the Realm. This would explain the mimicked dialogue between the long-deceased Louis of Hungary, defender of

Meeting of St. Paul the Hermit and St. Anthony. Fresco in the stucco fronton above the portal in the north aisle of the Basilica. 17th and 18th centuries

Christendom against the Turks, and his Chancellor, the Duke of Opole, founder and benefactor of the Paulite Monastery at Jasna Góra, who wished to confer their power and authority into the worthy hands of the anonymous figure of this man, who was to continue their mission. The most likely date of the endowment was about 1635. The picture may have been a thanksgiving offering for the chancellorship which had just been conferred on Zamoyski. The painter should be sought among the artists working for Tomasz Zamoyski at the time. In view of the characteristic brushwork, the only artist who can be seriously considered is Tomaso Dolabella who had left Venice to settle permanently in Cracow and become court-painter to the Polish branch of the Vasa Dynasty. The artist probably painted himself and his family among the group of pilgrims in the left-hand corner of the picture. The composition has yet another symbolic significance: its focal point, the Relic of St. Paul the Hermit, connects distant Venice, the artist's native city with the kneeling group of pilgrims, and on the other hand links the royal castle in Buda and the King, with the person who commissioned the picture, Tomasz Zamoyski, heir to the traditions of Christendom's defence against the Turks, and protector of the Paulite Order in Poland.

Coffin Portraits and Epitaphs

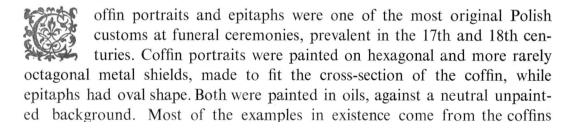 offin portraits and epitaphs were one of the most original Polish customs at funeral ceremonies, prevalent in the 17th and 18th centuries. Coffin portraits were painted on hexagonal and more rarely octagonal metal shields, made to fit the cross-section of the coffin, while epitaphs had oval shape. Both were painted in oils, against a neutral unpainted background. Most of the examples in existence come from the coffins

of great nobles, country gentry and the clergy, only occasionally from those of rich burghers. Usually, only the head and shoulders were represented, occasionally, the figure down to the waist, shown at an angle. Great care was taken for the likenesses to be as close to the original as possible. The lifelike expression of the eyes which seem to follow the viewer, help to increase this impression. The warm colours, generally used also helped to serve this purpose. Most of the coffin portraits in existence come from Great Poland, Pomerania, the Lubusz and Sandomierz regions, Eastern Little Poland and Mazovia. In the 17th century, the portraits usually measured 40 by 45 cm. but in the 18th century they became larger, up to 71 by 72 cm. in fact. Epitaphs are slightly smaller. Coffin portraits and epitaphs often displayed a high standard of art, despite the fact that they were usually the work of anonymous local painters, belonging to the guild. Frequently they were copies of portraits made in the lifetime of the deceased, limited to the head and shoulders.

The origins of this unusual custom have not been established to everybody's satisfaction, but it is undoubtedly one of the most characteristic features of Sarmatian culture and habits. The theory is that the custom of coffin portraits originated from the laicisation of medieval epitaphs. By giving the portraits the greatest possible resemblance to the original, the artists aimed to centre attention on the face. The practice began in the 16th century and attained its peak in the mid-17th century, when Sarmatian ideology, the ideology of the ruling nobility, was at its height. It was closely connected with the extreme pomp and ceremony of funeral rites, which were the absolute rule in Poland at the time and only died down during the Enlightenment period.

Foreign visitors describing the magnificence of funeral rites in Poland, related that " ... one was under the impression of attending a triumph rather than assisting at a funeral." The concept of the triumph of death, represented in Polish Baroque art with all its glamour and extravagance, was well suited to Sarmatian tastes. Funeral pomp and ceremony in Baroque style resembled a theatrical show, organised with great skill and at vast expense. The ceremonies continued for days on end. The extravagance of those funeral rites was further increased by medieval tradition and the strong influence exerted

Coffin portrait of an unidentified man in breast-plate armour and cape. 2nd half of the 17th century. The Arsenal

Funeral portrait probably representing King John III Sobieski. End of the 17th century. The Arsenal

Coffin portrait of an unidentified old man. End of the 17th century. The Arsenal

Coffin portrait of an unidentified man resembling that of Sobieski. End of the 17th century. The Arsenal

Funeral portrait of Jerzy Lubomirski, Palatine of Cracow, deceased in 1726. The Arsenal

Coffin portrait of an unidentified ecclesiastic with the "Poraj" coat of arms. 2nd half of the 18th century. The Arsenal

Coffin plate of Anna Eufemia Denhoff, née Radziwiłł, d. 1663. The Arsenal

by Italian, or rather Roman funeral ceremonial. As a rule funeral ceremonies took place several months after death, since a long time was needed for the preparations.

Laid in his coffin, the deceased played the principal role in those "theatricals." The coffin was laid on a magnificent catafalque, raised specially for the occasion in the centre of the church, known as the "castrum doloris." The portrait of the deceased, painted on a metal shield, was placed in the head of the coffin, or suspended from the canopy of the catafalque, in which case the portrait would be oval in shape. The likeness of the deceased, always represented as a living person, was the focal point of the farewell ceremonies rendering homage to his memory. As a rule, during the actual funeral ceremony the portrait would be taken off the coffin or catafalque together with the heraldic shield and epitaph bearing his titles and proclaiming his deeds of valour and hung up in the church. Occasionally the funeral orations delivered at the "castrum doloris" were published in print. Father Ambroży Nieszporkowicz, who died in 1701, was renowned for his funeral orations. The orations he delivered at the funerals of members of the Męciński, Warszycki and Denhoff families, are preserved in print.

In view of its exceptional significance as a centre of religious cult, Jasna Góra was a frequent site of such funeral rites. Sepulchral crypts under the Chapel of Our Lady and Basilica contain the earthly remains of the monks as well as of many benefactors of the Monastery. It was also the general custom to have exequies and Requiem Masses said for the deceased for many years, sometimes requested even before their death.

Occasionally, when a person of importance died, many likenesses of him would be painted and sent to various churches requesting Requiem Masses to be said for his soul. This was probably the case with the obituary portraits of King John III Sobieski, who died in Wilanów in 1696. It is difficult to recognize the features of the hero of Vienna in the bloated features disfigured by suffering. No wonder therefore that coffin shields and portraits are to be found at Jasna Góra. Some of them were painted on silver, a rare thing in Poland. In view of the expense involved, few people could afford the luxury.

Diamond Robe from the miraculous
picture of Our Lady of Częstochowa.
The Treasury

Ruby Robe from the miraculous
picture of Our Lady of Częstochowa.
The Treasury

151

The collection of coffin portraits, shields and epitaphs at Jasna Góra adds greatly to our knowledge of this domain of art in Poland. The existing documents and literature concerning them makes it all the more interesting.

The collection consists of six portraits, six heraldic shields and four epitaphs. Originally coffin portraits were hung on the side walls of the presbytery. The inventory made in 1819, listed "several portraits of many benefactors, painted on silver shields" among other silver objects hanging on the walls of the Chapel of Our Lady.

The collection includes the portrait of an unknown man, wearing breastplate armour and cape with a large fur collar. The ornamental frame is decorated in a large flower design. The portrait is shaped in the form of

The Diamond Robe. Late Gothic ornament with the Figure of Christ carrying the Cross against a background of flowering vine and a sash with the name of Mary. 15th century

The Ruby Robe. *Patrona Hungariae*, late Renaissance ornament from about the mid-16th century, representing the Madonna and Child, Patron of Hungary. Transylvanian workmanship

152

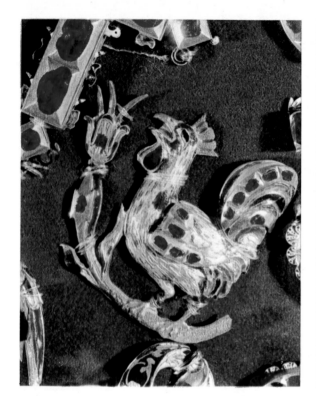

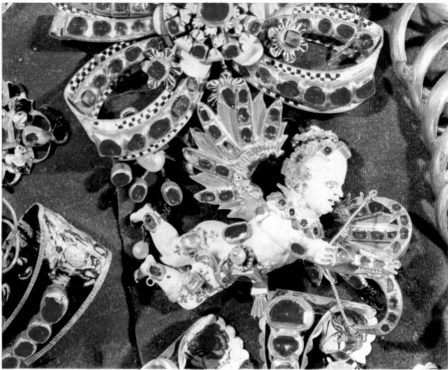

a horizontal rectangle, which seems to prove that it was painted in the second half of the 17th century.

Attention is drawn to the portrait of an unknown man with a flowing moustache, wearing a cape with a rich clasp at the neck. It is set in an oval, *repoussé* frame. The features closely resemble the portrait of John III Sobieski painted in 1690, now in the Wilanów Gallery. Considering the strong ties between the Sobieski family and Jasna Góra, and the King's great cult for the shrine, this may well be one of the obituary portraits of the Sobieski. Portraits in the "Sobieski style" were very popular in Sarmatian art at the

The Ruby Robe. A cock, probably a fragment of a larger ornament representing symbols of the Lord's Passion. Italian workmanship from the 2nd half of the 16th century

The Ruby Robe. Cupid ornament of Italian or German workmanship 17th century

154

17th century. The funeral portrait of an unknown man, very similar to the one described above, is an example of this kind.

The portrait of another unknown man dressed in sombre attire buttoned right up to the neck, also comes from the end of the 17th century. The wide well preserved frame with flower-design *repoussé* ornaments, creates an impression of magnificence testifying to the social rank of the deceased.

The funeral portrait of Jerzy Dominik Lubomirski, Voivode of Cracow, who died in 1726, is an outstanding example of Polish coffin paintings in the Jasna Góra collection. The portrait is almost a replica of the one in the National Museum in Warsaw. Attired in French costume and high, powdered wig, he is pictured wearing a fur-lined cape over a piece of light breast-plate armour. The frame, composed of six segments concealed at the joins by an ornamental design, is of imposing shape, with an intricate design in the French Regency style.

Jerzy Dominik Lubomirski was one of the greatest benefactors of the Jasna Góra Monastery. He contributed to the strength of the fortress, founding in 1720 the Bastion of St. Barbara, also known as the Lubomirski Bastion and in 1723 an imposing gate leading into the Monastery designed by the Silesian architect Jan Chrzciciel Limberger of Wrocław. No wonder therefore that his portrait is to be found in the Jasna Góra collection. It was probably dispatched to Jasna Góra after Lubomirski's death, accompanied by requests for prayers and masses to be said for the repose of his soul.

The more humble portrait of an unknown ecclesiastic with a Rose in his crest, dressed in characteristic Enlightenment period attire, probably comes from the second half of the 18th century. Ten coffin shields, four with epitaph inscriptions and six heraldic ones, also attract attention. All came from the sepulchral crypt of the Denhoff family.

So far, it has proved impossible to identify any of the three Denhoff family coffin portraits.

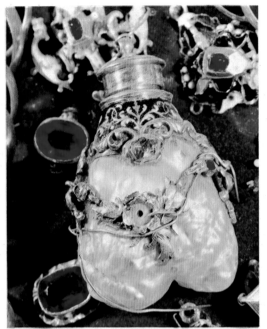

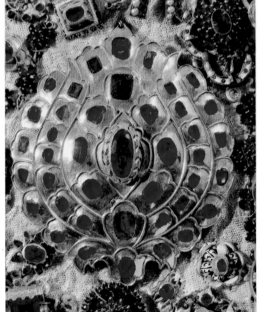

The Ruby Robe. A fisherman, ornament of Italian 17th century workmanship

The Ruby Robe. Ornament from a horse's harness 17th century workmanship, Turkish

Perfume flask made from a huge twin-pearl, 3 centimetres in length, without the setting. Italian workmanship from before 1731

The Diamond Robe. Central link of a chain, probably from the offering of Queen Maria Casimira d'Arquien-Sobieska. French or Transylvanian workmanship, 2nd half of the 17th century

The Diamond Robe. Early Baroque ornament in the shape of a winged heart with a black cupid. 1st half of the 17th century probably of German workmanship

Ornaments of the Picture of Our Lady of Częstochowa

IEWED against the background of the history of the picture, the ornaments belonging to it represent a separate problem for scholars. Of enormous value, they are not only a priceless collection of votive offerings but also a unique collection of national, historical heirlooms, complete with archive documentation. Many of the persons who offered the various pieces of jewellery, are known to us by name. Polish kings and the foremost dignitaries of the Realm figure among them.

The dark fascinating features of the Madonna of Częstochowa are always pictured with the heavy crown and glittering jewelled robe. The picture has been reproduced countless times. Some copies bear little resemblance to the original.

In the early centuries the ornaments were very different from what they are now. They extended over the background of the painting behind the Madonna and Child, leaving the faces and figures free, except for diadems over their heads. In fact the ornaments were a sort of silver and gilt extension of the frame, richly decorated and set in precious stones, in the manner typical of Eastern icons. The custom of adorning the picture with jewelled votive offerings took root in the 15th century. Necklaces, gold chains and brooches set with precious stones were fixed directly on the board of the picture, and in time, the figures were almost completely covered in jewellery. As more and more precious offerings kept flowing in they were placed in special cabinets on either side of the altar.

The robes were given their present aspect in the second half of the 17th century. The jewels were fixed on to a stiff velvet material and the robes were given a shape analogous to the outline of the figures of the Madonna and Child. Velvet is not a very lasting material, hence the robes had to be altered every now and again. Each time the jewellery was sown on again in a different arrangement and occasionally new pieces were added. Each of the robes is known by a different name. Their detailed description is to be found in the Monastery archives. The most valuable is the Diamond and the Ruby robe. The pieces of jewellery date from between the late 15th and the end of the 19th century. Nearly every piece is a work of art and some are truly outstanding, the oldest ones being Gothic. Some pieces are of Hungarian, West European and Eastern origin, the rest is probably the work of Polish jewellers, all the more interesting to art historians since similar pieces are almost nonexistent in other collections. In the light of recent studies, the votive robes of the picture of Our Lady of Częstochowa come to light as a unique collection, composed, one might say, of preserved fragments of our national history.

Old Weapons in the Jasna Góra Treasury

THE custom of presenting votive offerings to the picture of Our Lady of Częstochowa took firm roots in the 15th century. In the first half of the 17th century objects of lay provenance began to make an appearance alongside votive tablets, jewellery, liturgical vestments and accessories. They included magnificent weapons, trophies of war as well as insignia of rank and office presented by famous military commanders representing great historical and intrinsic value. In the first half of the 17th century such gifts acquired special eloquence in view of the resurgence of the concept of fighting the "Infidel," the foe of Christianity, identified at the time with the Ottoman Turks, who were a very real threat to Poland. The picture of Our Lady of Częstochowa had been raised to royal dignity in the reign of Władysław Jagiełło, but it was only during the period of the Vasa Kings that the cult of Our Lady of Częstochowa acquired real political significance. The Madonna of Częstochowa, victorious patron of the Polish chivalry, appeared on Polish banners at the victorious battles of Chocim (1621) and Beresteczko (1651). The defence of Jasna Góra against the Swedes only a few years later, in 1665, became a symbol of Christianity's victorious defence against heresy. In the second half of the 17th century it was the general con-

 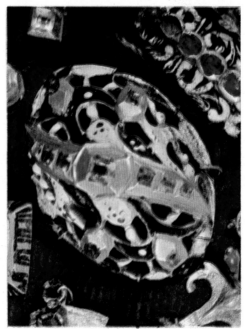 

The Diamond Robe. Baroque clasp in the shape of a bee, probably of Polish workmanship. 17th century
The Diamond Robe. Ornamental button from a Polish nobleman's costume. Part of a set offered by King Sigismund III Vasa. Polish workmanship, 1st half of the 17th century
The Ruby Robe. Ornament in Mannerist style, in the shape of a winged heart topped by a crown. 16th/17th century
Ornament representing the Child Jesus as the Redeemer, bordered by symbols of the Lord's Passion, probably of Polish workmanship (Cracow), early 17th century

viction that victories of Polish arms were due to the personal intervention of Our Lady of Częstochowa, a conviction firmly established in Sarmatian minds, which reached its peak after Sobieski's victory over the Turks at Vienna in 1683. Poland's close neighbourhood with the Muslim world, the inevitable contacts with Muslim art and culture, were bound to exert influence on Polish 17th century art and Sarmatian tastes. Oriental weapons of every description were highly prized for their artistic and ornamental value. Weapons presented as votive offerings and preserved in the Jasna Góra Treasury include many specimens of 16th and 17th century oriental and oriental-type weapons of great value. A 16th century oriental broadsword with a highly decorative hilt, embossed with turquoise and gold-inlaid agates attracts particular attention. The downward sweep of its curved hand-guard ends in dragon heads. The blade is gold inlaid. According to tradition, it belonged to King Stephen

Batory. Another magnificent late 16th century oriental sabre, according to Monastery tradition, was offered by the famous Hetman Stanisław Żółkiewski. The hilt and guard are gold-inlaid and studded with precious stones, but the blade is missing. Monastery documents tell that the Paulite Monks offered the sabre to King John III Sobieski when he stopped at Jasna Góra on his way to the relief of Vienna. The King accepted the blade only, remarking that steel was all he needed on his way to war. So the blade was detached but the hilt and ornamental scabbard remain preserved in the Treasury.

After his victory at Vienna the King offered a large part of the booty in gratitude and thanksgiving to the Madonna of Częstochowa. The offering included numerous specimens of oriental weapons as well as material from Turkish tents, which was draped round miraculous picture. *Bulawas*, insignia of the Hetman's office and symbol of his rank, are a great rarity in the collection. There are five preserved at Jasna Góra. They too testify to the oriental fashion generally prevailing in 17th century Poland.

The most splendid, the votive offering of Stanisław Revera Potocki, Grand Hetman of the Realm, presented in 1655, is a magnificent specimen of oriental goldsmith art and comes from the late 16th century. The workmanship, studded with turquoise and gold-inlaid agates is similar to that of the Batory and Żółkiewski sabres. The *bulawa* offered by Marcin Kalinowski, Field Hetman of the Realm, in thanksgiving for his release from Tartar captivity in 1650, is very similar. It was made by Armenian goldsmiths settled permanently in Lvov, probably in the 17th century. The 17th century *bulawa* of Persian workmanship, the head made from a single piece of rock crystal set with precious stones, is the pride of the Jasna Góra collection. It was offered by Józef Potocki, Grand Hetman of the Realm and founder of the south-east bastion at Jasna Góra Fortress. He died in 1701.

The *bulawa* presented by Stanisław Jabłonowski, Grand Hetman of the Realm, who died in 1702, comes from the second half of the 17th century. Undoubtedly of Polish workmanship it is embossed in oriental fashion with turquoise but its Baroque ornaments are of European design. Another heirloom which historical events connected directly with Jasna Góra, is a *bulawa*

Sabre of King Stephan Batory. 16th century Persian workmanship. The Arsenal

Sabre presented by Hetman Stanisław Żółkiewski. 16th century Por-
sian workmanship

from about the middle of the 17th century, with Baroque ornaments which combine oriental and western elements, probably the work of Russian goldsmiths. It was presented by the Moscovite Tsar Aleksei to the Cossack military leader Tymoteusz Cieciura, whose envoys later offered it to King John Casimir in token of their acceptance of Polish suzerainty. The act of solemn homage took place in the Knights' Hall at Jasna Góra on February 5th, 1661. After the ceremony, the King laid it in votive offering at the foot of the miraculous picture.

The collection of military heirlooms was preserved in the Jasna Góra Treasury, thanks to which it escaped looting and dispersal. The priceless national heirlooms it contains are inseparably linked with our national history and testify to the splendid traditions of art and culture in Poland.

A Treatise Written in Embroidery...

LONGSIDE many other liturgical vestments of great value, the Treasury at Jasna Góra contains a unique set of vestments known as the "Krassowski Apparatus," which dates from between 1720 and 1728. It comprises a chasuble, two dalmatics and a cope, together with all other accessories of a priest's robes and the chalice dressing: a stole, maniple, velum, pall and corporal. The whole set or "apparatus" is made of heavy silk material, covered in embroidery and *appliqué* work in silk and velvet. The varied technique of the embroidery is of extremely high artistic standard, combining sculptural and pictorial effects. An intricate arrangement of ribbons carries inscriptions explaining each item of the composition. Tiny human figures, modelled with extreme precision resemble dolls attired in magnificent robes. The faces, arms and legs are moulded in wax with silk drawn over them, the features marked in coloured threads. They are sown on the background material in flat-stitch technique. The theme of this extraordinary "treatise" which could only have been conceived by a man of

Bulawa (Hetman's insignia of office) offered in 1655 by Stanisław Revera Potocki, Grand Hetman of the Realm. Late 16th century Persian workmanship. The Arsenal

Bulawa of Marcin Kalinowski, Field Hetman of the
Realm. Votive offering presented in thanksgiving for his liberation from Tartar captivity in 1650. 17th century
Lvov workmanship. The Ar-
senal

the Baroque period, is a lecture on the role of Mary, Virgin Mother of Christ, in the work of Redemption. The lecture is illustrated by extracts from the Old and New Testament and supplemented with complex symbolic scenes, which expand the composition symmetrically. The Treatise begins with the Annunciation, embroidered on the back of the chasuble. It continues on the two dalmatics, showing the Apocalyptic vision of the Lamb from the Book of Seven Seals and the Gates of Heaven. It ends with the figure of the Virgin Mary in the Apocalypse, trampling underfoot the dragon Satan. The scene is embroidered in embossed technique on the hood of the cope. The patriarchs: Abraham, Moses, Aaron and David grouped round the Arc of Covenant, awaiting the Coming of the Virgin Mary are shown below. The main theme of the Treatise is supplemented with symbolic scenes and verset inscriptions in ornamental cartouches. A cartouche with the dedication and Arms of the founder and author of the Treatise, Father Michał Krassowski, is seen at the bottom of the chasuble.

Little has been written so far about the donor of this "apparatus." We know that he was born about the year 1680, heir to the property of Ostromę-czyn. His family, of country-gentry stock had settled permanently in Podlasie. He completed his education at the Jagiellonian University round about 1696 and entered holy orders shortly after. He is next heard of as the local parish priest on his property at Siemiatycze in Podlasie. In 1717 he became Canon of Warsaw. Later he was Custodian of Wiślica and from 1729, Canon of Przemyśl. He spent the last years of his life in Rome, where he died after 1740. Canon Krassowski took an active interest in public affairs and was twice elected to the Seym. He is remembered for his many Church endowments. Among other things he converted the parish church in his property of Siemiatycze and left large legacies to the Paulite Monastery in Warsaw and the Church of St. Stanislaus Kostka in Rome. He also had literary ambitions, as proved by five short treatises on theology, he published between 1696 and 1729.

These laconic references tell us little about the nature of the man. His vivid, typically Sarmatian personality comes to life in the light of the correspondence,

Buława offered by Józef Potocki, Grand Hetman of the Realm (deceased in 1701). The head is shaped from a single lump of rock crystal, 17th century Persian workmanship. The Arsenal

Bulawa of Stanisław Jabłonowski, Grand Hetman of the Realm, deceased in 1702. Polish workmanship, 2nd half of the 17th century. The Arsenal

Bulawa of the Cossack Hetman Tymoteusz Cieciura, presented by King John Casimir on February 5th, 1661, after receiving the homage of Cossack envoys. Russian workmanship, 2nd half of the 17th century. The Arsenal

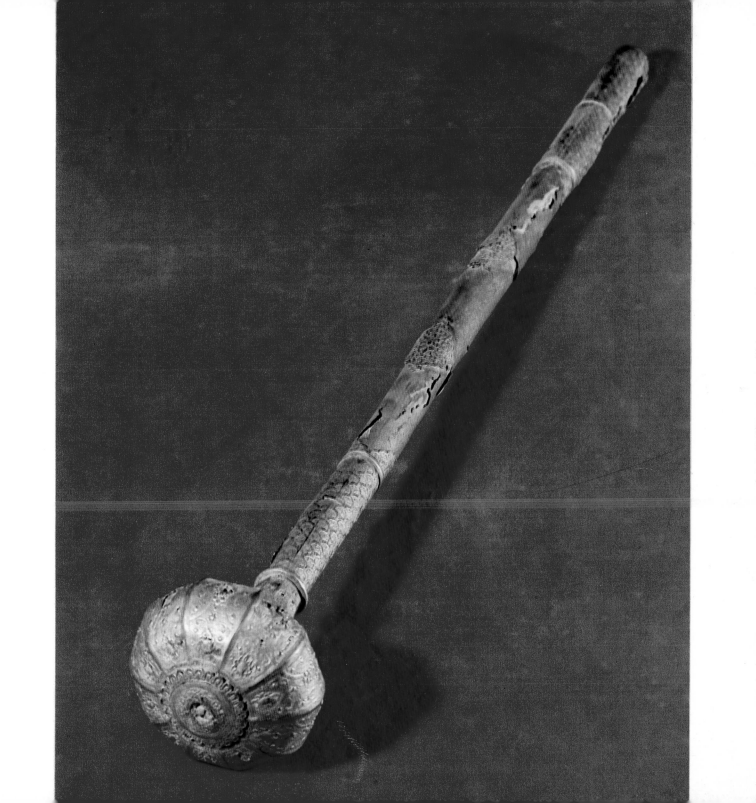

preserved in the Jasna Góra archives, which includes over forty letters addressed by the Canon to his close and dear friend, Father Konstanty Moszyński, Prior at Jasna Góra and Provincial of the Paulite Order in Poland.

Apart from devotional intentions, Krassowski nourished certain personal plans and ambitions when he offered this magnificent set of liturgical vestments to Jasna Góra Monastery. His correspondence discloses that for some years he had been vainly seeking Papal consent to publish a treatise discussing in detail the symbolic significance of Church vestments. In order to provide tangible evidence of the value of his treatise, Krassowski had two identical sets of liturgical vestments made, differing only in the text of the dedication. He offered one of the sets to Jasna Góra. In return for his generosity, Prior Moszyński consented to a hundred copies of the Polish and Latin versions of the treatise being printed unofficially in the Monastery press. The Canon set off for Rome taking with him the second set of vestments and several copies of the Latin version of his treatise, as an offering to Pope Benedict XIII (of the Orsini Family). In a letter full of Latinisms he wrote to Father Moszyński, he explains that " the apparatus was offered to the Holy Father on February 12th, 1726. His Aged Sanctity accepted it *summa satisfactione* (with the greatest satisfaction) ... "...Wearing his skull-cap only, he spent two hours and more, toying with details of the Apparatus, not omitting the inscriptions, and the mysteries discussed in the copy given him, or rather which he had ordered to be brought to him on first hearing news of my offering, which he reviewed and inspected, taking note of everything, standing at his table or walking back and forth, taking heed and observing everything, asking questions and answering them himself, discoursing at length on various details, easing his weak condition by constantly leaning his full weight on my arm, face to face with me. I might even say eye to eye, as an equal conversing with an equal and speaking with inexpressible pleasure."

Describing his audience with the Holy Father in greatest detail, Krassowski did not omit even culinary matters "... the Pope's lunch, served on two pewter dishes like the ones at Jasna Góra, consisted of broccoli and baked pastry. For dessert, he only took a piece of cheese — a true *Vita Apostolica*. Would that

Cope belonging to the "Apparatus" offered in 1726 by Father Michał Krassowski, Canon of Warsaw. Fragment showing the figure of Abraham. The Arsenal

we too could relish the example of the Apostle's Life and be judged worthy of the Eternal Supper."

Everything seemed to point to the fact that Krassowski's efforts to obtain Papal consent for the publication of his treatise were about to bear fruit, when the sudden illness and death of Benedict XIII, put an end to his hopes. Abandoning further efforts he returned home, leaving the magnificent "apparatus" in the Papal capital. In 1730 the Orsini, heirs of the Pope, offered it to the Chiesa dei Padri dell'Oratorio, one of the more important churches in Naples, where it is piously preserved to this day, together with a Latin copy of the treatise. An extensive essay on the "apparatus" by Father Antonio Bellucci, published in Naples in 1931, testifies to the undying interest aroused by it.

The Jasna Góra "apparatus" is still awaiting expert study. It is all the more interesting because Krassowski added another cope in 1728 but did not explain the theme of the embroidery in any written commentary. It seems he had already abandoned all hope of publishing his treatise and offered the copy for pious reasons only.

From the point of view of artistic value, both sets are outstanding examples of the art of embroidery in Poland. They are all the more valuable by virtue of the fact that the name of the donator and designer is known as well as the nuns who did the embroidery. They were Tertiary Sisters from Mienia in Podlasie, working under the direction of the Mother Superior Marianna Czermińska. The correspondence preserved disclosed that Canon Krassowski personally supervised the embroidering of every smallest detail of the "apparatus" to ensure it conformed with his design. He wrote repeatedly to Mother Czermińska, giving his instructions, amongs others that: "all the designs of the Cope, Chasuble and Dalmatics must be collected, and finally: should it prove expedient, and to ensure that no mistake is made, the completed work should be sent to me for inspection...". "We instruct you that the items which remain there should be preserved with the greatest care, so that the moths cannot get at them. Particularly the wools, for moths would make quick work of them." The history of Canon Krassowski's "apparatus", with which so many of his

Cope belonging to the Krassowski "Apparatus". Fragment showing Moses and the Burning Bush

hopes and ambitions were connected, provides most revealing material for experts studying the tastes and atmosphere of the Baroque period in Poland. To this typical representative of the Sarmatian period we are indebted for a work of art unique in Europe, unequalled in the richness of its form and significance.

Musical Instruments

 HE permanent exhibition in the Jasna Góra Arsenal also includes musical instruments, considered by experts to be of quite exceptional value. The exhibition includes the most valuable of the instruments preserved which had been used by the Jasna Góra musical chapel. The chapel, which gave both vocal and musical performance enjoyed a well merited reputation in Poland and abroad.

Documents testify to the likely contacts Jasna Góra entertained with other musical centres in the country, amongst others with Leszno, Łask, Łowicz, Kielce, Cracow and Wrocław as well as with centres abroad, such as Eisenstadt, Prague, Dresden and Vienna. Established in 1600 the orchestra continued in existence up to the outbreak of the First World War in 1914, longer in fact than any other musical group in Poland. Some eighteen hundred music compositions preserved in the Jasna Góra archives and the valuable collection of old musical instruments, testify to the scope of its activities. The orchestra was formed not only to meet the needs of religious cult, but for prestige reasons also. Numerous references to "solemn pomp" to be found in Monastery

Collection of musical instruments from the 17th to the 19th century, used by the Jasna Góra orchestra. The Arsenal

176

chronicles, provide some idea of what those solemn occasions were like. Visits by monarchs, Church and lay dignitaries provided occasion for solemn pomp and ceremony, as did funerals of prominent persons. Triumphant arches would be erected, monumental catafalques raised, firework displays, theatricals and recitals organised. All such occasions were accompanied by vocal and orchestral performances.

Originally, only the monks played in the Jasna Góra chapel. Soon however, laymen were also admitted. Usually they were peasants from villages belonging to the Monastery. "This time I am sending you four boys who play in the band in Siemiatycze," Michał Krassowski, Canon of Warsaw, wrote to Father Konstanty Moszyński in 1737. "You had better examine them personally, Honourable Father, to see whether they are suitable (...) should it prove to the contrary, please send them back to me as occasion offers. The two who are still here I will bring myself, and if you decide to keep any of them please see that they have no time to laze. Let them be occupied with Music, or the godly work of making church carpets..."

At first, only monks were the chapel's conductors, but from 1636 on, lay conductors were also employed. Soon, it became the custom to have two orchestra conductors at Jasna Góra : a monk and a layman. The conductor was responsible for the repertoire and the standard of playing. He also had the duty to watch over the moral behaviour of musicians. This duty often caused the conductor considerable trouble: unconcernedly, musicians would repeatedly pawn their instruments in Częstochowa pubs. Occasionally they would vanish for days to the great shock and annoyance of the worthy fathers.

No picture of musical life in Poland would be complete without a history of the Jasna Góra chapel. Dr Paweł Podejko, a musicologist from the Poznań School, has conducted laborious research into the history of the orchestra and has published some excellent works on it. Amongst others he succeeded in ascertaining the names of 371 musicians who played in the orchestra from the 17th to the end of the 19th century, and included twenty-eight composers. The 156 musical pieces co posed by them and preserved in the Jasna Góra archives, are mostly unknown. Many of the compositions show a high musical standard, and should find a place in the repertoire of old-music ensembles at the earliest opportunity.

The archives also contain a valuable collection of 18th and 19th century musical scores, numbering some eighteen hundred items in all. The collection would have been far larger had it not been for the fire in 1690, which destroyed the older musical manuscripts together with the 17th century interior of the Basilica.

Among the many musical instruments used at Jasna Góra and dating from the 17th to the 19th century, some are very rare indeed. Foremost among them are several slender, natural high-pitched trumpets, tuned to a very high key (clarino). The oldest one is of Prague workmanship, bearing the maker's signature EK on it. It was made at the turn of the 16th century. Another, also of Prague workmanship was made by Jan Bauer in the 17th century. A Nuremberg clarinet, made by Hieronimus Starck, dated 1693, is a European rarity. Among the many wind instruments dating from the 16th to the 19th century, a valve trumpet for the left hand made by Augustus Wolf about the year 1800, is particularly noteworthy. Such instruments were made only during a period of fifteen years, hence they are a great rarity in world collections. Among the string instruments, special attention must be drawn to a bass-viola, made in 1771 by the German violin-maker Ignatius Hoffmann.

Thanks to the foresight and care of the Paulite Monks, the instruments used at Jasna Góra have been preserved in good condition. The collection has great interest value for all lovers and students of music.